Living to Die, Dying to Live

Living to Die, Dying to Live

An Exit Strategy for Institutional Christianity

MICHAEL W. SHIREY

WIPF & STOCK · Eugene, Oregon

LIVING TO DIE, DYING TO LIVE
An Exit Strategy for Institutional Christianity

Wipf & Stock
An Imprint of Wipf and Stock Publishers
199 W. 8th Ave., Suite 3
Eugene, OR 97401

www.wipfandstock.com

PAPERBACK ISBN: 978-1-5326-9648-0
HARDCOVER ISBN: 978-1-5326-9649-7
EBOOK ISBN: 978-1-5326-9650-3

Manufactured in the U.S.A.   10/01/19

This book is dedicated to my father, John E. Shirey,
without whose weekly conversations and constant support
it would not have been written. He is a blessing
to aspiring writers all over the world, including me.

There is a time for everything,
and a season for every activity under the heavens:
a time to be born and a time to die,
a time to plant and a time to uproot,
a time to kill and a time to heal,
a time to tear down and a time to build,
a time to weep and a time to laugh,
a time to mourn and a time to dance,
a time to scatter stones and a time to gather them,
a time to embrace and a time to refrain from embracing,
a time to search and a time to give up,
a time to keep and a time to throw away,
a time to tear and a time to mend,
a time to be silent and a time to speak,
a time to love and a time to hate,
a time for war and a time for peace.

Eccl 3:1–8, NIV

Contents

Preface

If all goes according to plan, this book will make you mad. I state that without apology. It is not the book I set out to write a decade ago when I embarked upon a sabbatical to explore the Jewishness of Jesus and how it relates to modern Christianity. I did write that book but, frankly, it did not deserve to see the light of day. Then in 2017 my wife and I received the gift of a trip to the Holy Land where we spent two weeks walking in the footsteps of Jesus. It was a life-changing experience, one that led me down a path I never expected to travel. I learned that faith is a visceral experience, not a set of doctrines to which one must subscribe. Jesus lived, breathed, and walked the earth. He spoke to people, meaningfully interacted with them, and—most of all—declared that God wanted to be in a deeply personal relationship with them.

This is still true today. There are those who declare that Christianity, at least in the West, is dying. They are right in one respect and wrong in another. One must make a clear distinction between institutional Christianity and the vibrant, organic faith that Jesus and his followers established and which still lives. It may be overshadowed by groups that claim to have a lock on the truth and essence of the gospel, but it persists, most often in those places where it is forced to exist in the shadows. In contrast, the institution that grew up around that faith is teetering on the brink of extinction, which is not a problem in my view. In fact, it will be good for the overall health and survival of the Jesus movement. Institutional Christianity, as I will define it, has done much good in the world, but it is time for it to step aside and allow followers of Jesus to do what he wants them to do.

This book is different from those that seek to define and diagnose what is wrong with modern Christianity and offer a solution. I am writing not from the halls of academia, but from the frontlines of ministry. I have spent thirty years in the trenches, serving churches in the heart of the Midwest with no influence in the highest levels of their national organization and little voice in their local communities. My solution rejects everything associated with institutionalism and advocates a return to the earliest formulation of Christian existence. I predict that few will be ready or willing to consider it, but I believe it to be the true solution, nonetheless.

If I haven't scared you away, and if you are willing to embark on this journey with me, then please keep reading. Otherwise, see if you can get a refund, or pass this book on to someone you believe might appreciate it. In any case, pray for the ongoing health of the Jesus movement. One way or another, the end is near, and we need to be ready.

Acknowledgements

I want to acknowledge, first, my wife Marje for her patience and support as I have worked to make this book a reality. She is my soulmate in every sense that matters. My parents, John and Barbara Shirey, supported me faithfully through my late teens and early twenties as I tried to figure out what God wanted me to do with my life. They hung in there as I wandered from religion to religion and state to state, never giving up on me, and I thank them for their support. My brother David and my sister Kathy have been a big part of making this book happen, for which I am and will be forever grateful. Special thanks to the late Rev. Dr. Roane Deckert, who rescued me from the darkness of ministerial despair and helped me see that serving Jesus could still be a joyful and fulfilling experience. Among those who read the initial drafts, I want to thank Terry Towery and Rich Kruiswyk for provided helpful comments. I also want to thank Rev. Dr. Doug Hucke for arranging for the sabbatical that started me down the path of writing a book. Christine Bollwinkle and Mike and Paula Brattin generously helped me with the cost of publication. The credit goes to all of those I have mentioned—the mistakes are mine alone.

Introduction

How do you respond when someone tells you not to do something? My high school creative writing teacher began our first class by telling us about a student who had chosen death as the subject of his assignments. The teacher stated that it did not go well. I do not know if he intended it to be a challenge, but I decided to do the same, turning in assignments that included death in some form. The teacher did not penalize me, apparently because I handled it well and was neither morbid nor suicidal. I discovered a flair for creative writing that I did not pursue until later in life, to my regret. My rebellious moment resulted in exemplary grades in that class, but my superior academic performance in that area did not extend to my other classes or to the remainder of my time in high school. And my fascination with death soon turned into a deep and sometimes debilitating fear of dying. Death became something I tried to avoid thinking about at all.

My efforts to avoid thoughts of death were futile, as I subconsciously knew would be the case. I have since discerned that death is a reality to be embraced—not in a suicidal sense, but as a natural part of human existence. The ancients understood this far better than do we who live in these supposedly enlightened times. While we typically equate death only with the end of life, it pervades every aspect of our reality, including the customs and institutions we create. Death is as inevitable for institutions as it is for people. Yet, we do not deal with institutional death in the same way that we deal with the death of human beings. As callous and harsh as it may be, the death of the elderly is natural in that it makes room for the newly born. In the same way, the death of an institution can make way for something new and better. This is the case with institutional Christianity, which has existed for more than sixteen centuries, leading some to believe that it will be around forever—or at least until Jesus returns. I do not believe that this is either true or necessary. The institutions and organizations in the Western world that claim to be the descendants of the original Jesus movement have strayed from their mandate, becoming less effective in the process. Self-preservation is more important to them than selfless service that may lead to torture, imprisonment, and death. This is tragic given that Christianity is founded on the assertion that death is nothing more than the door to new life. There is almost unanimous consent among scholars that institutional Christianity in the West is dying. I submit that this is a good thing because it must die if it is to live. Its future life is found only in death.

It is easy for me to be cynical about the future of the institutional church. While on the one hand there is no other institution that I have loved more fervently, served more diligently, or that has played a greater role in my more than half-century of life, on the other hand no other institution has done more emotional and spiritual harm to me and brought me deeper disappointments than the strange beast called institutional Christianity. I have seriously considered giving up on the church and even abandoning my faith at least twice. It was not until I was doing the research for this book that I realized that faith in Jesus does not depend on the institutions claiming to be founded in his name to accomplish his purpose and complete his mission. In fact, as I hope will be made clear by the end of this book, whenever the institution believes it is indispensable to the work of salvation, it is time for that institution to die.

Christianity in the Western world is dying. The question is not how we stop it. Instead, we need to ask why it is happening and how we should respond. In my opinion, institutional Christianity must die so that the message Jesus intended for his followers to share with the world can be clearly heard once more, stripped of all the institutional and political nonsense that has accrued to it over the years. Death is the only hope of new life, and Christianity, rather than formulating a plan for survival, must instead formulate an exit strategy, dying so that it can live and accomplish the purpose for which Jesus called it into being.

This book was written from the frontlines, not the halls of academia. Twenty-eight years as a pastor in several different states and contexts do not make me an expert, but they do allow me to make a credible report from the battlefield. These are thoughts and reflections, nothing more, but perhaps they will stimulate some conversation, or at least some honesty from both pastors and parishioners, about why the church in the Western world is in such a dismal state. I do not have a detailed solution, but I believe I know what needs to happen after the last shovel of dirt is cast onto the grave of institutional Christianity. Where there is life, there is hope, but where there is faith in Jesus, there is the hope of eternal life in the face of death in every form. Read on, and perhaps you will find hope for the future of this strange thing we call Christianity.

Chapter 1

A World Without Religion

Religion is the sigh of the oppressed creature, the heart of a heartless world, and the soul of soulless conditions. It is the opium of the people.

—Karl Marx[1]

What would the world be like without religion? Would it better or worse? This is a fiercely debated question. Atheists and agnostics have become more vocal in their assertion that religion has no legitimate place in the modern world. This is not new. Karl Marx (1818–1883) believed religion had no use except as a means of keeping people docile and easily controlled. Some of Marx's ideological descendants enthusiastically support the eradication of religion. They point to countless examples of misery and oppression perpetrated in the name of religion, the decadence and hypocrisy of religious leaders, and the vast wealth and possessions institutional religions accumulate even as they exhort their adherents to sacrificially donate their hard-earned money in the name of advancing the stated mission of the institution. Further, they add, all religious belief is just superstitious nonsense. Then there are those who are critical of religion in general but still believe that it can be of some use in the world once "religious extremists" are silenced.

There is no clear way to answer the question regarding the relative benefit or harm caused by religion without first attempting to define it. I have chosen for the sake of argument to define religion as an institutional system of doctrines and practices designed to regulate and govern matters of belief and behavior for a group or groups of like-minded people. Religious institutions are concerned with matters of theology,[2] which is one reason

1. https://www.brainyquote.com/quotes/karl_marx_402037.
2. Basically, the study of God and how God relates to the world.

why Marx, who believed all theology was outmoded and should give way to modern philosophy, dismissed religion as no longer relevant to society. Marx was also an atheist, which did not improve his view of religion or his hostility toward it. Given his philosophical views, he probably did not have much use for religious faith in any form. This is interesting given that Marx was ethnically Jewish, the grandson of a Dutch rabbi, and was baptized Lutheran. His encounter with liberal humanism in high school undoubtedly contributed to his attitudes toward religion. Marx was not a fan of religion, but religious institutions could benefit from studying his ideas about the benefits of a classless society, nonetheless.

My intent is to draw a clear line between religion and faith based on my view that while religion *can* be the external manifestation of faith, faith does not need a formal religious structure to express it. Making this distinction requires some deep thinking about the difference between religious belief and religious practice. Unfortunately, the line separating them is blurred by shallow thinking, rigid preconceptions, and deep prejudices. Ideally it should be possible to offer a critique of formal religion as distinct from personal faith, but in practice this requires more effort than the average person is willing to devote to the task. While some religions are regarded with tolerance and relatively free from attack except by extremists, Christianity in all its expressions is fair game in the modern world. Some criticism is justified, coming as it does in response to authoritative statements Christians make in areas that have little or nothing to do with matters of faith or, worse yet, twisting the words of the Bible to promote political causes. The most obvious example is in the arena of social justice. This is a valid concern, but within the realm of Christian faith it is a compassion issue, one that has nothing to do with politics. But I digress.

Many who publicly express negative opinions about organized religion shy away from overt criticism of Islam, sometimes choosing to characterize it as more of a faith than a religious institution. This is a fair assessment given that there is no single living Muslim leader to whom all of Islam looks for authoritative guidance. Just as there are multiple "Christianities," so are there multiple "Islams" all vying for supremacy to varying degrees. The elephant in the room is the fact that Muslim extremists, much like Christian extremists in the not-too-distant past, do not easily tolerate criticism, thereby inadvertently shielding all of Islam from serious criticism. This is a gross generalization, but it seems to me that Islam is where Christianity was about five hundred years ago. The problem is that what was tolerated then is utterly intolerable now. At the same time, Islam has much to teach Christianity about its past actions and present belief, if we will but take the time to listen. Dialogue is possible, but only if all parties are willing to set aside the ludicrous notion that all religions are equally true or even that all religions contain some but not all truth. Religions are fallible because they are human constructs. The most fallible of them are the ones that become institutions. If religion is to be effective it must support the expression of faith, not dictate what doctrines must constitute that faith. Personal faith existed before organized religion and seemed to get along just fine without it.[3]

A world entirely without religion would be strange indeed, but a world without *institutional* religion would have its advantages. Chief among them is that faith would flourish without the artificial restrictions imposed upon it by people claiming to have an exclusive lock on the truth in all matters pertaining to life and death. Organized religions have been and continue to be their own worst enemies, deserving a fair portion of the criticism directed against them. Without judging whether it was better or worse, it is fair to say that religion in ancient times was localized, personal, and informal. Personal faith was just that—personal—and judged to be more important than formal rituals. Ancient religious thought and practice was centered around family and tribal deities whose perceived duty was to protect, provide for, and ensure the fertility of womb and field for their worshippers. Not until religions became intertwined with national identity and tied to the coercive power of the state did significant problems begin to arise. Nationalistic religions reared their ugly heads early in human history. Few religions have resisted the clarion call to ally with the state and harness its power in their efforts to enforce religious doctrines and practices.

Institutional religion has been around a long time, but that does not make it either necessary or inevitable. Judaism and Christianity both had a pre-institutional period when they existed apart from nationalistic claims. Judaism succumbed to institutionalism a thousand years before the time of Jesus when a lowly shepherd boy named David from an insignificant family in a minor tribe managed to unite the twelve fractious Israelite tribes into a cohesive nation. Largely for political reasons, he established Jerusalem as the political and religious capital of Israel. This marked the symbiotic joining of religion and state. Christianity followed suit three centuries after the death of Jesus, succumbing to the siren song of nationalism after having existed until then as a loosely connected coalition of regional groups of congregations centered in Rome, Alexandria, Antioch, and Jerusalem. Arguments about doctrinal issues were frequent, but only infrequently resulted in more than isolated physical violence. That changed after Christianity became the official, state-sanctioned religion of the Roman Empire. Nationalistic religions are fraught with dangers, not the least of which is the

---

3. The divine encounters in Genesis 1–35 make this clear.

temptation to enforce conversion at the point of a sword. Islam is different in that it began life closely tied to a political movement aimed at uniting the disparate Arab tribes to face a real military threat.[4] Nationalistic religions become dangerous when they adopt a "convert or die" mentality—a danger the founders of the United States sought to avoid. Despite their best efforts, American Christianity has tried to rewrite history and make it seem like their intent was to create a "Christian nation." This is far from the truth, and that is a charitable assessment.

> Congress shall make no law respecting an establishment of religion, or prohibiting the free exercise thereof. . .
>
> —US CONSTITUTION, AMENDMENT I

I inwardly cringe whenever I hear the United States of America referred to as a Christian nation. Christianity may still be the dominant religion in America (at least nominally) but some of the values an increasing number of Americans hold dear do not align with basic Christian beliefs and principles. This is not a *political* problem given that the founders of this nation did not intend Christianity to be the official, or the only, religion practiced by its citizens. They tried to create a nation where all religions are welcome, and all are free to practice their faith without interference from the government. After all, they or their forebears had recently escaped from a nation that persecuted anyone who dared resist whatever the state religion happened to be at the time. Some of the founders were Deists and Freemasons[5] who publicly paid lip service to Christianity when it was deemed necessary but did not adhere to many Christian beliefs or accept that all the stories in the Bible are true. The founders did not want the United States to have a state religion, but their descendants failed to pay attention, eventually establishing Protestant Christianities (unofficially) as the dominant religious expression in the nation. Roman Catholics faced localized persecutions, but Protestants eventually grudgingly accepted them as fellow Christians in the face of increasing challenges by atheism and secularism (i.e., the enemy of my enemy is my friend). Other groups and individuals who attempted to redefine or reform Christian belief and practice were not so fortunate. Read about the outrages committed against Mormons, Jehovah's Witnesses, and several Baptist groups by "established" Christian religions to see that this is true.[6]

4. A good history of the origins of Islam can be found in Armstrong, *Muhammad*.

5. I do not have a problem with Deism or Freemasonry, especially given that some of my ancestors were Masons and that I was a Mason for a few years. My point is that the founders were familiar with religious persecution and wanted to create a place where everyone, even deists and freemasons, could freely worship.

6. One great source is McGrath, *Christianity's Dangerous Idea*.

Institutional religions can be problematic. But is eliminating them the correct response to the damage they have done and continue doing in the world? The question *can* be answered if we start by understanding that it is an organizational rather than a philosophical concern. We must separate institutional questions about correct doctrine from philosophical questions about the existence of a god or gods. This is an important distinction: Divine beings are not created by religious institutions. Instead, religious institutions exist because of a perceived need to codify and regulate what it means to believe in and live in relation to a divine being or beings. It therefore stands to reason that those who deny the existence of divine beings see no purpose in the continuing existence of religious institutions. Since it is impossible to empirically prove or disprove the existence of divine beings (despite all attempts to do so), the best approach is to focus on the institutions that claim to exist to serve such beings. This is easy enough to do given some understanding of the institution's origins, mission, and purpose. It can be argued that only those within the institution can accurately evaluate it, and while that may be somewhat true, those on the outside are free to judge whether an institution is acting according to its publicly stated goals. Since this already happens regarding Christianity, why not apply it to all religions as well?

Some religions have come under fire for questioning the prevailing opinions and beliefs of the culture in which they exist. A few have fought back while others have quietly acquiesced. All try to define themselves in response to cultural pressures, whether in support of or in opposition to them. Institutional religions at every point along the ideological spectrum attempt to codify belief, doctrine, and practice for two reasons: First, it lets them to distinguish themselves from other religions for purposes of membership recruitment and hoped-for cultural influence. Second, it lets them claim, if they choose, the exclusive right to decide how one should live in the present and what happens when one dies. Some progressive religions exclude those who do not subscribe to a doctrine of indiscriminate inclusiveness, which is as Orwellian as you can imagine. The proliferation of religions has resulted in a proliferation of exclusive claims, many of which are in direct opposition to one another. This creates confusion for anyone seeking religious answers to important questions. It is the cause of criticism and derision by those who have no use for institutional religion. As was true when the movement that became Christianity was born, there are a plethora of philosophical alternatives to religion that do not entail burdensome financial, behavioral, or time commitments while also allowing one to sleep in on the weekend.

> Religion is a system of wishful illusions together with a disavowal of reality, such as we find nowhere else but in a state of blissful

hallucinatory confusion. Religion's eleventh commandment is
"Thou shalt not question."

—Sigmund Freud[7]

Any serious attempt to define religion raises questions: Are religions
human constructs or divine institutions? If the latter, then which one is
right? Maybe all are right and were established by multiple deities so that
humans would have options because, after all, variety is the spice of life.
Is religion in general, as Sigmund Freud (1856–1939) opined, "a system
of wishful illusions together with a disavowal of reality"? Since the Age of
Enlightenment (1715–1789), scholars, scientists, and philosophers have
claimed that advancement of human knowledge has eliminated the need for
religion. In their opinion, humanity has outgrown the need for divine over-
seers other than as distant entities who may step in to save us from complete
destruction at the appropriate moment. They assert that ancient human beings created religion to explain phenomena that they lacked the scientific
knowledge to understand and incorporate into their worldview. Science,
the opponents of religion argue, eliminated the need for all superstition,
especially religion. As Karl Marx might say, there is not enough room in the
world for both science and religion. The past must give way to the present if
there is to be any hope of achieving the utopian society to which all humanity should aspire. Religion stands in the way of progress.

I do not entirely disagree with this assessment. However, that statement comes with a caveat: it is a valid assessment only when applied to institutional religion as distinct from personal faith. Religion and faith can and
do overlap but properly belong to different facets of the spiritual experience.
Religion is a human attempt to express divine realities through carefully established rules and rituals. Faith does not depend on institutions. Religious
institutions help faith develop, but just as often get in the way of meaningful spiritual growth. Many of the classes I attended in churches as an adult
(and some of those I led) were surface level, filled with pleasant platitudes,
but rarely challenging. A friend recently told me that when he offered a
theologically deep answer to a question posed by another person in a class
he was attending, the leader told him that such answers were inappropriate
because he did not want to scare away visitors who could be intimidated by
the fact that they might need to learn something that was intellectually challenging to be a follower of Jesus. This is illustrative of a systemic problem in
the religious institution.

7. https://www.brainyquote.com/quotes/sigmund_freud_13917.

Freud characterized religion as a system, which is true, but only part of the picture. Religion can also be described as a universal phenomenon, one that embraces every age, race, culture, and region of the world. Institutional religions have existed in one form or another for as long as people have created organized systems to define the parameters of the relationship between divine and human beings. Speaking in general terms, while religious institutions have always existed, so too have skeptics, doubters, deniers and disbelievers. This is good when viewed as an opportunity for religious people to define, explain, and defend their beliefs, hopefully leading to a clearer understanding of them. It is bad when religious people use it as an excuse to hound, condemn, and persecute those with whom they disagree. I do not condemn, nor do I have a problem with, those who sincerely question the validity of religion so long as a clear distinction is made between religion and faith. It is possible to be a person of faith without being religious (I have not always agreed with that statement.) The reverse is also true: it is possible to be a "faithful" religious person without having faith (I have observed this many times.) I know people who have given up on organized religion for various reasons, but still claim to be spiritual, which for them means a general, undefined belief in God that (conveniently) does not include personal sacrifice or involvement in a church. I have also known people who were deeply involved in the life of a local church, but whose words and actions betrayed a complete lack of faith in anything they claimed to believe. There are also pastors who privately disavow everything they publicly claim to believe so they can keep their jobs, seminary not having prepared them for any other career.

> "I like your Christ, I do not like your Christians. Your Christians are so unlike your Christ."
>
> —MAHATMA GANDHI[8]

Questions about the necessity of religion in the Western world tend to focus on one specific, multifaceted religion. Modern Christianity in its various expressions has found itself on the receiving end of overt criticism since at least the 1960s. This is particularly true for Christian groups on the fundamentalist side of the spectrum. Many of these groups are dying off (some more quickly than others) because they refuse to accept that the days are long past when it was possible to browbeat someone into a "conversion experience" by threatening eternal damnation. Part of the reason for this is that few people of any religious persuasion acknowledge the existence of a place of eternal punishment called hell, and those who are not religious reject

8. Attributed to Gandhi, but this is disputed. See https://en.wikiquote.org/wiki/Mahatma_Gandhi.

it out of hand. Some who are willing to consider the possibility believe that not many will end up there, one's eternal destiny being a matter of choice rather than judgment. This has inexorably led to the rise of Christianities that are more concerned with cultural acceptance and social justice than with helping people live faithfully in the present while preparing for life in eternity. In parts of the Western world Christianity has become little more than a loosely, often badly, organized collection of advocacy groups support- ing various causes, some of which are in direct opposition to beliefs long espoused by Christians throughout the history of the Jesus movement. Add to this the plethora of sexual abuse and misconduct scandals that have come to light across the ideological spectrum and it is easy to see why Christian- ity in the West has come in for its share of criticism. Priests, pastors, and other leaders have used their positions to coerce children, youth, and adults into performing acts in private that they publicly denounced from the pulpit. There is no possible way to justify these actions. My sympathies are entirely with the victims. The only question I have, one that others have asked, is as to whether their actions invalidate the mission and the message with which Jesus entrusted his followers. Christianity, like religion in general, has been its own worst enemy.

Judgment day will not be a pleasant experience for some who claimed to have acted in the name of Christ. The quote attributed to Mahatma Gan- dhi concerning Christ and Christians nicely captures this sentiment. Many Christians, among them a depressingly large number of people in positions of leadership, have brought disrepute to the words of Jesus through their actions and inaction. Gandhi, being a Hindu, did not believe the asser- tions of the Bible about Jesus and was naturally looking for valid reasons to reject them. He easily found them in the hypocritical actions of those claiming to be followers of Jesus. In Gandhi's opinion, Christians routinely disproved the validity of their faith in Jesus by their actions. Hinduism has been around a long time, originating around 2000 BC[9], but it is as much a way of life as it is a religion, which may be why the lifestyle advocated and modeled by Jesus appealed to Gandhi even if the institution that grew up around that way of life did not. There is religion, and then there is faith. If faith and religion are identical, then religion, despite its flaws, is necessary and the world would certainly be adversely impacted by its absence. If faith and religion are independent of one another, as I believe, then faith can and will survive the death of religions—indeed it will thrive and grow in the absence of institutional structures. The religious institution in the Western world called Christianity is terminally ill. Most Christian organizations in

9. The roots of modern Judaism go back to around 1800 BC.

existence today will survive another generation or so in their current form, but their epitaphs have already been written and their graves already dug. The only thing left to do is hire the preachers and prepare the services. Yet, there is hope for Christian faith as distinct from institutional Christianity if it is willing to travel the path that leads through death to life.

> Persecution is as necessary to religion as pruning to an orchard.
>
> —AUSTIN O'MALLEY[10]

I find it fascinating that the places in the world where Christians are a persecuted minority are also the places where personal faith is strongest. Christians in America may disingenuously claim persecution by pointing to unflattering portrayals in the movies, on television and in other media, and to efforts to remove religious monuments from public spaces, but until we endure actual torture, imprisonment, and death because of our beliefs, what we are experiencing is a minor inconvenience, not legitimate persecution. So long as we are free to spend millions building and maintaining luxurious church campuses and contributing to causes that do not require us to get our hands dirty or interact with people in desperate need, we are not being persecuted in any meaningful way. Criticism is helpful to the cause in that it helps us identify the message the world is hearing from us. If we pay attention, we will discover that it is not often the message we think we are conveying. Characterizing criticism as persecution is catering to the desires of the non-believing world in the interests of inclusion, tolerance, and relevance: three words that have been hijacked by radicals who are using them to delegitimize the essential message of Christianity.

Religious institutions come and go, but faith remains. Institutions rarely stay the same over time even if they manage to maintain an outer façade that appears to be unchanging. Roman Catholicism is one example. Centuries-old cathedrals and churches are still in use, but the rituals observed in them differ significantly from the ones used by the earliest Christians. The same is true of Protestantism. Faith in Jesus is eternal, but institutional Christianity will not survive beyond the end of human history. The institution will die, but faith will survive the demise because there are Christian movements in the world that will keep on going when it happens. The future of Christianity is not in the trendy mega-churches that court the affluent and preach a "lite" version of the gospel. Instead, the future of Christianity is in the third world, mostly Pentecostal churches that challenge the values of the culture and work to provide hands-on help and hope to the poor, oppressed, and downtrodden. My hope is that the Christian religious institution in the

---

10. http://www.notable-quotes.com/o/omalley_austin.html.

Western world will die with a bang rather than a whimper, standing firm in the face of the real persecution that will surely come one day. My fear is that it will continue to adopt non-Christian values and eventually fade away due to decreasing relevance and increasing competition from organizations that do the social justice thing with far greater efficiency and competence. This has already happened in Europe and is well underway in America.

While I strongly suspect that no one reading these words will live to see the complete demise of religion in the world, I believe that we will live long enough to see a radical restructuring of the Christianity in the West. If utopia-minded theorists are correct, humanity is destined to evolve beyond the need for religion and the guidance of divine beings. Science fiction writers over the years have imagined what such a world might look like. Most of the portrayals are dystopian, but perhaps they are wrong in their negative assessment of human potential. Fear not: religion will survive into the foreseeable future. Institutional Christianity is another matter; it is at a pivotal moment, not for the first time and perhaps not for the last. Radicalism, fundamentalism, reform, and cultural accommodation are struggling for supremacy, recognition, or tolerance. It is important to realize that Christianity has been at this point more than once over the last two thousand years. The first generations of Jesus followers faced the same problems as they struggled against persecution and the pressure to compromise their values to conform to the culture. The same forces are at work today. Changes are taking place in the institutions that claim a connection to a first century Jewish preacher and teacher named Jesus as they struggle to understand their role in the modern world. It seems like the institution, at least as it has been traditionally understood, is on the verge of extinction. The question is not how we can prevent it, but how are going to deal with it and what is going to happen when it is over.

> All national institutions of churches, whether Jewish, Christian, or Turkish, appear to me no other than human inventions set up to terrify and enslave mankind, and monopolize power and profit.
>
> —THOMAS PAINE[11]

My faith as I have lived it for more than five decades has had its fair share of crisis moments. Several times I believed that I was on the brink of losing my faith entirely. Twice in the past dozen years I found myself wondering if Christianity had any validity for me whatsoever. I walked back from the edge the first time because I had a job to do, a family to support, and only a few months to contemplate my churning thoughts. Most recently, I was blessed

---

11. https://www.brainyquote.com/quotes/thomas_paine_401915.

to able to spend nine months studying Christianity and my relationship to it in the past, present, and future without working in a church. I realized that my faith in Jesus was not the issue; instead, it was my faith in the institution. I was born and baptized into the Roman Catholic Church and spent four years studying for the priesthood. I devoted another three years to studying for the ministry as a Presbyterian. I have served churches in four different states and two Presbyterian denominations over the past twenty-eight years. Somewhere in all of that I lost my faith in institutional religion but, thankfully, not my faith in God and devotion to Jesus. They have survived, but much of what I learned over the years as incontrovertible doctrine is suspect in my mind even though I have taught it in the sincere belief that it was correct. My problem is that efforts to promote one doctrine over another, one set of beliefs over another, and one hierarchical structure over another have led to the deaths of countless Christians at the hands of other Christians since at least the fourth century AD, something I believe brings Jesus to tears.

Religion is a human construct built and governed by fallible human beings. It can never legitimately claim to be a fully divine institution. Faith is hope and trust in "things not seen"[12] and exists independent of human institutions. Some label it as superstition, others imaginative delusion, and those are two of the kindest labels. Religions are created and destroyed, the evidence of their existence being a matter of historical record. Faith, on the other hand, defies proof or disproof; it is an exercise of the will. It involves, as the writer of Hebrews asserted, "the assurance of things hoped for, the conviction of things not seen." Critics consider it foolish to believe in what cannot be seen, yet every breath depends upon an unseen element. Air can be measured, and its physical existence confirmed, but that does not make it any less unseen. Faith is like air; both must be experienced to have any benefit. I experience air by taking it into my lungs and I live because of it. I experience faith by relying on its object and living it out according to my beliefs about what it entails, and I hope for eternal life because of it. Faith does not require a building, rituals, laws, or leaders. This is one reason why it will survive the demise of organized religion.

> The good news is there's no devil. The bad news is there's no heaven. There's nothing.
>
> —KERRY PACKER[13]

---

12. "Now faith is the assurance of things hoped for, the conviction of things not seen" (Heb 11:1).

13. https://www.brainyquote.com/quotes/kerry_packer_404230.

John Lennon once famously urged us to imagine a world without religion. Others, like the Australian businessman Kerry Packer, took it a step further and declared that religion is a farce because it focuses on what does not exist. I am willing to imagine a world without religion, but I hope it is clear by now that I am not talking about a world without faith. The places in the world where religion is suppressed, oppressed, and persecuted are dark and depressing, but faith survives precisely because its survival does not depend upon the existence of institutional religions. This is true in the case of every religion, not just Christianity, but Christianity has a long history of surviving during times of persecution, both official and unofficial. The first Christian communities that spread over the Roman Empire experienced sporadic persecution, some of it from isolated groups of Jewish leaders, some from Roman officials, and some from ordinary citizens. Reasons for persecution varied from group to group and place to place, but the single factor that united every dispersed group of Christians was the firm belief that faith in Jesus was a cause worthy of death regardless of who happened to be doing the persecuting. Compromise and accommodation were largely unthinkable (unlike today), and it was judged to be better to die for one's faith than deny or dilute it to prevent death. Christians did sometimes compromise in the face of threatened persecution, which created a controversy that lasted many decades. It would probably have been resolved amicably had not the church chosen that moment to ally itself to the state and gain for itself the ability to punish those with whom it disagreed instead of merely arguing with them. It was not the church's finest hour. Institutional Christianity is today reaping the putrid harvest of corrupt seeds sown centuries ago.

The modern world seems to be a dark and dismal place, yet it is sweetness and light when compared to what the world would be like without any form of religion. I am not suggesting that religion needs to go away. My point is that religion is like a ship that has gone off course and the crew doesn't know where it is heading. The following example may shed some light on what I am trying to say. I started a new job and needed to bring an old laptop that is several years old but still serviceable back into use. After booting it up and working with for a short time I realized that no amount of software maintenance was going to put it in working order. What was needed was a complete reinstall of the operating system. This is what I am advocating for Christianity. It is no longer enough to tweak doctrines, rituals, worship spaces, outreach strategies, or hierarchies. We need a complete reinstall of the operating system. We need to make a fresh start. It will not be easy because it involves death. Here's the question: Does Christianity have the courage to die so that a new reality can come to life? I hope so, but I fear that it will not happen. Regardless, the monster that we call Christianity is headed towards death, at least in its current form. What are we going to do about it? I am suggesting that we let the patient die, offer palliative care if necessary and appropriate, plan a funeral, and move into a new reality. As painful as it might be, we need to talk about death before we can talk about new life.

Chapter 2

Dearly Beloved, We Are Gathered Here Today . . .

> Your worm is your only emperor for a diet. We fat all creatures
> else to fat us, and we fat ourselves for maggots. Your fat king and
> your lean beggar is but variable service, two dishes, but to one
> table. That's the end.
>
> —HAMLET, ACT IV, SCENE III

Death is the great equalizer. When all is said and done everyone born into this world ends up as a feast for maggots. Morbid? Perhaps, but many problems in the world can be boiled down to lack of respect for death. I have some experience in this, having conducted over two hundred funerals in the past three decades. Some of them went well, others were less than memorable, but each taught me something. Several failed attempts to portray unsavory characters in the best possible light taught me that the best funerals are not the ones that paint a picture of the deceased as the nicest, most generous, and saintliest person who ever lived—a description that usually departs at least a few degrees from reality. Instead, the best funerals are the ones that allow family and friends to acknowledge, accept, and begin to adapt to an unchangeable reality that no longer includes the one who has died. One reason many people struggle to deal with death is that it cannot be changed, avoided, or denied. Rich or poor, powerful or helpless, famous or unknown, death takes us all. The increasing preference for cremation, based more on cost than anything else, is gradually changing the way people deal with death. There is something undeniably final about holding an urn containing the ashes of a loved one. Denial is sometimes easier when the deceased is made to look as if he or she is "just sleeping" whenever a family requests a "viewing" of a loved one as part of the services, but the reality is that death is the end of existence in this world, no matter how hard we try to escape it or deny it.

Many in the Western world do not like death, the one exception being when it is used in some form of entertainment, be it a movie, a novel, a television drama, or a video game. People fear death because it is the last and greatest unknown. This fear has grown in reverse proportion to the decline of deeply held religious belief in the Western world. The ancients dreaded death, as we do today, but also accepted it as part of the life cycle of the world; they knew that it could not be avoided indefinitely. In fact, given the right circumstances, death was an honor to be sought (especially in battle), not a tragedy to be avoided. Some cultures even regarded the act of suicide with a measure of respect. The ancients who gave it any thought were more concerned with how best to influence what happened after death than with the act of dying. They acknowledged death as an inescapable reality of human existence even as they mourned it loudly and extravagantly, sometimes paying professional mourners to carry on excessively at the funeral. This is still true in some cultures today. Persistent denial of the reality of death is not healthy. Once accepted as inescapable, death gives life a richness and sense of purpose that it might not have otherwise. Death is inevitable but does not have to be debilitating. It can and should bring meaning to life. If nothing else, it provides those who must deal with the death of a loved one the chance to reflect, learn, and grow. The best funerals embrace this reality and help the living adjust to an irrevocably altered existence with a healthy amount of grief, but also with renewed hope.

> To fear death, gentlemen, is no other than to think oneself wise when one is not, to think one knows what one does not know. No one knows whether death may not be the greatest of all blessings for a man, yet men fear it as if they knew that it is the greatest of evils.
>
> —SOCRATES[1]

The older I get, the more funerals I find myself attending. Funerals tend to follow a basic pattern and I have long since learned how to respond appropriately. But the events leading up to a funeral are as varied as life itself, which means that my response varies depending on the nature and depth of my relationship with the deceased and his or her family, the circumstances of the death, and the spiritual needs of those impacted by it. I am not sure which is more painful: watching a beloved family member die or watching

---

1. http://www.searchquotes.com/Socrates/Death/quotes.

as others watch a beloved family member die, hoping that they do not blame me for failing to cure them through prayer. I have been in both places. There are plenty of clichés available for such situations, and I have used all of them at one time or another. All the talk of "being free from suffering" and "going to a better place" may bring a measure of comfort but does little to lessen the reality of death. I have observed that the process of dying is often far easier for the one facing death than it is for the ones who stand by and watch it happen. I spent my first ten years as a pastor working in churches and communities that were predominantly elderly, so I conducted my share of funerals. The funeral homes in the first two communities I served as an ordained pastor were owned by members of the church I served, and I conducted funerals for families who "needed a pastor" because they did not belong to a local church or were nominally Christian at best. Interaction with those families taught me that non-believers generally understand the reality of death more deeply than believers, even if they do not want to accept it; they mourn it intensely because of the sense of utter finality they attach to it. My point is that until and unless you are willing to deal with the finality of death, you will have no real appreciation for what life has to offer and, perhaps more importantly, why it is so important to be concerned about what happens after you die.

I have been pondering all of this recently, but in relation to an age-old organization rather than a person: institutional Christianity, by which I mean the host of established groups, both large and small, of Christians organized around sets of beliefs, doctrines, and forms of governance. This list includes Roman Catholics, Protestants, Mormons, Jehovah's Witnesses, and any other group that looks to Jesus as the central figure of their faith. Some will argue with this list, but I do not believe anyone has the authority to decide who is or is not Christian. A Christian is a follower of Jesus. Period. Mere human beings do not have the authority to tell anyone who can and cannot follow Jesus. This is not to say that every denomination and independent church is equally right, but rather to say that all of them are wrong insofar as they claim to possess the only complete understanding of Jesus' message. That ship sailed three centuries after Jesus of Nazareth died on a Roman cross outside the occupied city of Jerusalem, when an organic movement began changing into a static institution by entering into an unholy alliance with an emperor who saw Christianity as a tool that could be used to unite a widely dispersed, diverse empire. This was problematic in part because there were multiple Christianities at that point, although only two of them were positioned to influence events outside of their local communities. The emperor supported one side in public but adhered to the other in private. He did this because Christianity was more important to him as a political tool than as a means of spiritual nurture and support.

The emperor supported the faction he believed most capable of helping him bring religious peace and unity to the empire. The irony is that the emperor and the ascendant Christian faction used each other to achieve their goals, which despite public statements to the contrary, rarely had anything to do with ensuring the spiritual health of the faithful. Instead, they appeared to be far more concerned with political control than with the spiritual comfort of the people.

The institutional Christianity of which I am speaking was born in AD 325 at a place called Nicaea, during a church council called by an emperor who cared less for discerning spiritual truth than consolidating his empire around one religion. The outcome was less than satisfactory. To put it in modern terms, the "liberals" defeated the "conservatives" at Nicaea and gained ascendancy, but the losing side did not go quietly into the night. A truly monolithic Christianity has never existed, except perhaps in the first few decades of the Jesus movement's life on the streets of Jerusalem. Instead, there have always been Christianities—disparate groups whose uniting factor is a focus on Jesus as their founder and the determiner of their beliefs and actions. These groups divided, united, ebbed, and flowed over time, adapting to changing political, cultural, and philosophical movements, and participating to varying degrees in the conquest of Europe and the lands that came to be known as the Americas. Unfortunately, the spread of Christianity, while successful in terms of numerical growth, was plagued by internecine warfare and fratricide that resulted in countless self-inflicted wounds. Christians killing Christians is never okay, and it is utterly heinous when done in the name of enforcing "correct" doctrine. The struggle for doctrinal, and at times political, supremacy created a cancer within the body of institutional Christianity, one whose presence is only now emerging fully into the light: the demonic belief that leaders within the institutions are not bound by the ethics and morality they impose on others.

> "Our age knows better. . ... What was formerly merely sickly now becomes indecent—it is indecent to be a Christian today."
>
> —FRIEDRICH NIETZSCHE[2]

Nietzsche's words were published over a century ago (1895) but are even more relevant than when they first appeared, although perhaps for different reasons. They are of a piece with his judgment that Christianity is weak, irrelevant, and anti-intellectual, hence his statement that "it is indecent to be a Christian today." The religious landscape in the West was

2. https://www.goodreads.com/quotes/740287-our-age-knows-better-what-was-formerly-merely-sickly-now.

becoming increasingly secularized by the end of the nineteenth century. Mainline Christianities were devoting more focus and effort to social justice concerns and political activism than spiritual matters. Nietzsche did not see these efforts as a positive because he believed they were born out of pity and therefore catered to weakness. In his view, pity preserves and increases misery by creating a sense of dependency, something for which he had no patience. Nietzsche believed that this was Christianity's weakness, a weakness that it made it indecent in modern society. Is that assessment still true today? I believe so, but perhaps not in the sense that Nietzsche intended.

I believe that Christian indecency as Nietzsche defined it is another form of the cancer growing in the body of institutional Christianity. It is the cancer of conformity to cultural norms at the expense of fidelity to the message. Briefly stated, Jesus' message is "Repent and believe the gospel." The message of institutional Christianity is "accept and acquiesce to the culture." Some take a middle ground, attempting to "update" the gospel message to appeal to a new generation, but this too is doomed to failure. The gospel, as Nietzsche rightly discerned, is counter-cultural, which is why he dismissed it as irrelevant and indecent. There was no room in his philosophy for helping the hurting or being compassionate to those in need in a physical sense, let alone in a spiritual one. I wonder if he would have had more respect for Christians if they had been willing to stand up to the prevailing secular notion that religion was becoming irrelevant in an increasingly rationalistic world. The message of the gospel is indecent because it dares to suggest that the rich help the poor, the strong help the weak, those who are healthy take care of the sick, and that no one seek to be lord and master over another. When the epitaph of institutional Christianity is written, will it include the assertion that it was indecently caring and recklessly compassionate, or will it be judged to be irrelevant to anything that truly matters?

Christians *are* judged to be indecent, although not always in a positive sense. Leaders who use their position of authority to abuse children are indecent in the classical sense of the term. They deserve any and every punishment heaped upon them. Yet there are also Christians who are judged to be indecent if they dare challenge or question the prevailing cultural assertions regarding ethics, morality, and the like. The responses are varied but can be boiled down to two: accept the judgment and live into it by challenging prevailing cultural notions or seek to change the judgment by conforming to cultural expectations. In either case, the outcome is often, but not always, organizational death. My experience is that some churches take the middle ground by ignoring the extremes and providing their members with a bland approach to faith that offers little help dealing with major challenges. These churches may not be dying as fast as those on the extremes, but they are dying. At some point soon, the money will run out, the plug will be pulled, and that will be the end. No human institution is eternal, not even institutional religions.

Secular pundits and religious scholars alike solemnly declare that mainline, institutional Christianities are no longer relevant and are slowly but surely dying. Since they often have little or no practical experience on the front lines their opinions are best taken with a grain or less of salt. Yet, there is some truth to what they claim. Christianity in the West is terminally ill; it seems likely to die. Some will mourn the loss, some will profess not care, and some will respond with a hearty "Good riddance!" I confess that I find myself in each of these camps frequently, sometimes simultaneously. Institutional Christianity will die because it is a human construct, not a divine creation, and therefore riddled with faults and fallibilities. Every human institution suffers from this malady. Problems arise when religious institutions claim to be divinely established, infallible, eternal, and imbued with the sole power and authority to deliver definitive divine instructions to the world. It is vital that we distinguish between the "church" as Jesus of Nazareth envisioned it and the bureaucratic behemoth called "Christianity" that was cobbled together in his name centuries after he left. The church, as distinguished from institutional Christianities, is a living organism that the New Testament describes as the body of Christ. There is much about that term that we could unpack, and countless scholars have done so, but my purpose in bringing it up is to point to it as proof that the earliest Jesus followers viewed the church as a movement first and only then, if at all, thought about it as an institution.

The church is the body of Christ, which means that it is the embodiment of Jesus and his mission and therefore cannot and will not die. The institution can, will, and should die for the good of the church and its mission. This death is neither altogether positive nor negative, although it will be perceived by some as one or the other. Those who mourn the death of the institution will legitimately point to the countless lives it has positively impacted during its tumultuous two millennia-long life. Followers of Jesus working in service to the institution have accomplished many wonderful things throughout history and even into the present. This must not be denied, but it is mostly the stuff of comforting eulogies. Christians have selflessly put their lives on the line to care for victims of plagues and other illnesses, shelter the persecuted and oppressed, and work to better living conditions in some of the most destitute regions of the world. At the same time, some will greet the demise of the institution with little sorrow and perhaps even some gladness, pointing to the incredible damage it has inflicted on millions of people, including fellow followers of Jesus, all over the world. The list is long, depressing, and growing longer. Both sides have a valid point.

None of this is easy for me to ponder or to write. I have spent more than half my life—over three decades—preparing for or engaged in serving churches both large and small in the Midwest and Southwest. This does not make me an expert on institutional Christianity, but I do believe it gives me some perspective on the problems Christianity faces today, particularly in this corner of the globe called the United States of America. Mainline institutional Christianity *is* dying in the United States of America. It is already dead in Europe except for a few places where it is on life support, most notably Rome. Yet even in the heart of the Roman Catholic Church institutional loyalty tends to trump personal faith in Jesus, as may be seen from the official responses to the latest disgorging of sexual abuse accusations by the hierarchy. While the Western church limps along suffering from self-inflicted wounds, Christians in other parts of the world face increasing violence.[3] Despite persecution, small, often independent, churches are flourishing underground in many of those places for reasons most westerners fail to understand.[4] Let me be clear: Christianity will survive the demise of every institution in the world that claims to promote it. This has been true since the moment Jesus handed the baton to his followers on a wind-swept mountain in Jerusalem two millennia ago. The race is ongoing. It remains to be seen how it will be won.

Institutional Christianity is terminally ill, but must it die? Millions of words have been written attempting to diagnose the disease inflicting mainline institutional Christianity and how best to cure it. There is a simple answer, although it will be unacceptable to the experts who have built careers on detailed diagnoses and carefully constructed cures. Some propose fervent prayers for revival using methods set forth in a book or program they are trying to sell (I may be accused of the same thing.) Others suggest implementing strategies and programs modelled on those adopted by the non-religious corporate world. The former method has failed me given that my prayers for healing have gone unanswered as often than they have been answered. As to the latter, frankly, I did not enter pastoral ministry to be a corporate drone. I have been involved in many different programs and read dozens of books designed to build an efficient disciple producing machine, none of which have ever had any deep or lasting impact on the health of the institution.

> Ninety-nine percent of everything that goes on in most Christian churches has nothing whatsoever to do with the actual religion. Intelligent people all notice this sooner or later, and they conclude that the entire one hundred percent

---

3. China, North Korea, and the Middle East are just a few examples.
4. Africa and South America, among other so-called "Third World" nations.

is bullshit, which is why atheism is connected with being intelligent in people's minds.

—NEAL STEPHENSON[5]

Far too many churches are guilty of spreading bullshit instead of bringing people into a deep and meaningful encounter with Jesus. Does that statement offend you? If so, then you will want to pay close attention when we get to chapter 7. There are exceptions to every rule, and I will be forever grateful to those who stood by me over the years, made the effort to grow in their faith, and worked to rise above the fray of petty church politics, which is the source of much of the garbage in local churches. Unfortunately, most of them did not have the means, either socially or financially, to influence or impact the direction of the institution. The unacknowledged but tacitly accepted truth is that money governs the direction of the church far more than does faith and spiritual conviction. Ego has something to do with it as well. People who would otherwise have no means of attaining the highest standing in the local community find that they can gain recognition by rising to the highest levels in the church to which they belong. This is amplified when wealth and influence are brought to bear on church governance. One of the biggest obstacles to church growth is the attitudes and intentions of the people who agitate the most for church growth. Far too often their goal, stated or not, is to increase the number of people putting money in the offering plate, not increasing membership in the kingdom of God—although they characterize their efforts as such. They will take full credit for any positive gains while blaming the pastor for any perceived losses in any area of the life of the church—including finances.

This is one reason pastors love to complain about church members when they are with other clergy. It can reach Olympic-level competitiveness when pastors gather for meetings and conferences. Some church members want their pastor to be Jesus. Most pastors are happy if most of their congregation is at least nominally Christian. While that may seem harsh, it has been my experience that just as pastors enter and stay in the ministry for a variety of reasons, so people join churches for different reasons. Institutional churches are filled with imperfect people, as is every human organization. This is not the reason the church is sick and dying. People who are still "seeking a church home" (not one of my favorite phrases) are as often as not looking to fill a need they may not even be able to clearly describe. The suggestion that an institution can be a spiritual home is fraught with danger, implying as it does that spiritual satisfaction can be found in a

5. https://www.azquotes.com/author/14089-Neal_Stephenson.

fallible, finite, temporal human construct. Institutional Christianity is dying because it is trying to satisfy spiritual hunger with the wrong kind of food. But many people are also seeking the wrong kind of spiritual food. They want spiritual fast food: entertaining programs, something fun for the kids, and Bible teaching that supports what they already believe. Churches fail these hungry spiritual seekers when they acquiesce to their ill-conceived demands in the name of filling seats and meeting the operating budget. While it may be an exaggeration to assert that "ninety-nine percent of everything that goes on in most Christian churches has nothing whatsoever to do with the actual religion," it is fair to say that a great deal of what happens in the name of "running the church" has little or nothing to do with furthering the cause of Christ and proclaiming the gospel, as much as church leaders might claim otherwise.

> "If your ministry can't work without you, then it is no longer Christ-centered. Minister toward Jesus, not yourself."
>
> —REV. KELLEN ROGGENBUCK[6]

Pastors struggle not to yield to the temptation to blame all the problems of the church on the people in the pews, often with limited success. It does not seem to matter whether the pastor is deeply spiritual, deeply cynical, or somewhere in between. The blame is always at least partially misplaced in part because pastors, like the imperfect people they serve, are human and therefore just as imperfect. While it can be helpful to try to diagnose a church's illness by looking for the source of the disease elsewhere, in more than a few cases pastors will find the source of the problem by the simple expedient of taking a long, hard look in the mirror, as I have done. They will discover that they are part of the problem because they are far fuller of themselves than they are of anything truly spiritual. Pastors of every stripe in every denomination and religion must stop believing that they are indispensable. A seminary education can do more harm than good. I have seen it happen more than once. Seminaries that train pastors for service in institutional Christianity are often as cut off from reality as are many college and university campuses in America. Aspiring pastors' heads are filled with high-blown theological concepts and notions about the Bible that are not only inaccessible to the average person in the pew but are also patently unnecessary. The enter active ministry believing that is their "call" to educate the ignorant masses clinging desperately to their outdated beliefs and quaint traditions, when in fact all they really need to do is help people understand what it means to love, follow, and serve Jesus.

6. https://www.goodreads.com/author/quotes/15236576.Rev_Kellen_Roggenbuck.

Many pastors graduate from seminary believing it is their job to "save the church from itself" by preaching and teaching whatever useful truths they can glean from the Bible. Those who have the right connections serve in churches that help launch them up the career ladder to a larger, more affluent church. Those who do not find themselves serving small churches in small communities where they soon discover that most of what they learned in seminary is completely useless. The ones who try to educate their congregation according to their seminary indoctrination soon find themselves out of a job—I have seen this happen more than once. More than a few give up and leave ministry entirely. Some do whatever it takes to retain their position while striving to appear successful according to the standards of the world. I have watched with disgust as pastors jostled for position at meetings, looking down at anyone who did not fit their definition of what it means to be a member of the professional clergy. They flaunt their technological superiority by ostentatiously making sure everyone sees them using the latest and greatest electronic devices while flashing the latest books written by all the right authors and not deigning to be governed by schedules and agendas they did not personally set. They routinely leave meetings to check with their church because, after all, it cannot possibly operate efficiently without their oversight.

Classism and elitism are alive and well in institutional Christianity. Nearly every pastor has a story to tell about affluent church members who flaunted their success in subtle but obvious ways and met socially only with those of their own class while less-affluent members harbored resentment in their hearts and, because they knew envy was wrong, struggled to grow in their faith. Divisions are accentuated when pastors openly seek the favor of the wealthiest church members, hoping for a share of the crumbs that fall from their well-provisioned tables. At the same time, many churches intentionally or unintentionally impoverish their pastors, claiming that pastors should not be serving the church for financial gain because they are "working for the Lord." Meanwhile, they spend the resources of the church on worldly endeavors. After all, new carpet in the sanctuary is far more important than ensuring that the pastor is making enough to support his or her family. Installing the latest technology is more important than making sure those in need, the people Jesus called our "neighbors," have food to eat and clothes to wear.

> "The institutions of Churchianity are not Christianity. An institution is a good thing if it is second; immediately an institution recognizes itself it becomes the dominating factor."
>
> —OSWALD CHAMBERS[7]

Here is what I know: Christianity as an organic movement, as a living faith, will survive the death of the institutional church. It was a movement long before it was an institution, in those heady days when the first followers of Jesus finally understood what he wanted them to do and then actively set out to do it. I submit that the Jesus movement will be better, healthier, and far stronger following the death of institutional Christianity because, in part, the institution demands conformity to a prescribed set of doctrines and dogmas while the movement asks only for simple faithfulness and dedication to the cause. Christians will survive the demise of the institutional church because they existed and were carrying out their mission long before power-hungry ecclesiastics got it into their heads to try and make everyone toe the same line. We must never forget that Jesus does not need an institution to accomplish his ultimate mission. Christianity flourished and spread after the institutional church was chased out of and mostly disappeared from Asia, Africa, and now Europe. The same will undoubtedly be true when the last flickering flame of institutional Christianity in the USA is finally extinguished by the dank, fetid winds of secularism. It is fascinating to me that the gospel is finding its way back powerfully into the places where the church was first born and grew into maturity.

I do not know much, but I do know that Jesus did not die so that his followers could form a bureaucracy-laden institution. Jesus died so that those who truly believe in him can share eternity with him. The institution saves no one, and never has, all past and present claims notwithstanding. One could reasonably argue that the movement Jesus started during a three-year ministry in the cities and villages that surround the Sea of Galilee no longer exists. It died with the last of his original followers near the end of what we now know as the first century AD. There are those who believe that what we call Christianity began life as a religion invented and spread by Saul of Tarsus, better known to the world as the apostle Paul, whose writings fill more than half of what we call the New Testament. I would suggest that Paul did not intend to start a new religion even though that is effectively what happened. He almost single-handedly delivered to the non-Jewish world an incredible message about a Jewish Messiah who had been crucified and resurrected for the salvation of Jew and non-Jew alike. Paul's efforts focused primarily on Greek-speaking non-Jews in Asia Minor, many of whom had

7. https://www.azquotes.com/quote/416212.

little practical knowledge of Judaism. Regardless of his intentions, which are impossible to recover, the direction, drive, and focus of his most zealous followers resulted in a hybrid religion composed of Jewish belief and Greek philosophy. A careful examination of the history of Christianity clearly shows that there has never been a monolithic Christian Church. There have always been and continue to be multiple Christianities, each with its own set of doctrines and code of behaviors. All these movements began as a sincere attempt to reform the institutional church as it existed at the time and, in turn, each fell victim to the temptation to institutionalize.

I do not claim to be an expert on church renewal or revitalization. My sermons, Bible classes, and devotions have been well-received, but by-and-large, while individuals have grown, the churches I served did not increase appreciably in either size or faithfulness. In fact, each of the churches I served experienced an overall decline in membership during my time with them. This was due to a combination of factors including attrition by death (I conducted over two hundred funerals in twenty-seven years), loss of families through transfer or relocation, the decline of mainline churches in general, and dissatisfaction with my ministry or that of the head pastor. One of my greatest strengths, according to those who have observed me in action, is the ability to deliver a powerful eulogy and provide comfort to families grieving the loss of a loved one. I have neither the learning nor the authority to offer a solution to the problems facing Christianity in the present age. Instead, I stand silently beside its bedside, composing the eulogy that I will be called upon to deliver when the loved one dies. I no longer offer prayers for healing because I no longer see any hope for recovery. I believe that the death of institutional Christianity will be a good thing because new life, resurrection life, will follow. My eulogy for institutional Christianity will celebrate what was good about the deceased. It will also identify the nature of the (mostly self-inflicted) wounds that led to its demise.

There are some who will assert that a eulogy for institutional Christianity is long overdue since the God it claims to worship and serve is already dead. Please note that this is different than saying that God does not exist. The former presumes that God once lived but is now dead, while the latter denies that God ever lived at all. If God is dead then the obvious question is, "How did God die?" And if God died, was it from natural causes or murder? If it was murder, then who is responsible for the deed? I think it was murder, and I believe I know who did it. The answer may or may not surprise you. Of course, before the "big reveal" we need to set the scene.

Chapter 3

Is God Really Dead?

> God is dead. God remains dead. And we have killed him. How shall we comfort ourselves, the murderers of all murderers? What was holiest and mightiest of all that the world has yet owned has bled to death under our knives: who will wipe this blood off us? What water is there for us to clean ourselves? What festivals of atonement, what sacred games shall we have to invent? Is not the greatness of this deed too great for us? Must we ourselves not become gods simply to appear worthy of it?
>
> —Friedrich Nietzsche, *The Gay Science* [1]

I wonder what the weather was like when the April 8, 1966 edition of *Time* magazine hit the stands provocatively asking, "Is God Dead?" Apart from meteorological conditions, it was by all accounts a stormy time in the United States of America. The façade of the American dream that the veterans of World War II carefully constructed upon their return from service was slowly but relentlessly crumbling. Life no longer seemed as certain as it was in the halcyon days of the 1950s. The violent winds that were sweeping across the political, religious, and cultural landscape of the nation spared no one, not even those at the pinnacle of society. John F. Kennedy had been assassinated three years earlier in Dallas, Texas on November 22, 1963. His brother Robert would follow him to the grave courtesy of an assassin's bullet on June 5, 1968. The Vietnam War was approaching its eleventh anniversary and still had nine years to go, but vocal public protests were escalating over what was increasingly perceived as American involvement in a largely foreign conflict. John Lennon had publicly declared a month earlier

---

1. https://www.goodreads.com/quotes/22827-god-is-dead-god-remains-dead-and-we-have-killed.

that the Beatles were more popular than Jesus (prompting some churches in Alabama to burn Beatles albums and memorabilia). The Civil Rights Movement in America was underway, and the assassination of Martin Luther King Jr. at the age of thirty-nine was almost exactly two years in the future, on April 4, 1968. Life seemed filled with uncertainty.

The 1960s were a turbulent time by every definition of the phrase. There was political and civil unrest all over the world. The Vietnam War was increasingly troublesome to many, especially given the ambiguity that had surrounded American involvement in the Korean conflict a decade earlier. The direct threats to American values and freedom posed by the world wars were relatively easy for the average person to grasp, but this was not the case with reference to Korea or Vietnam. Americans were finding their voices, to put it in modern terms. As is generally true of such periods, social, moral, political, and religious norms were being called into question; everything was fair game for public reevaluation. Nietzsche's question gained new life in this environment. Those who paid attention to its context realized that the question was especially relevant given its focus not on God's existence, but on whether God had anything meaningful left to say to humanity. In other words, had modern advancements in science, technology, and philosophy rendered God obsolete?

These are not new questions. They reappear at those pivotal moments when human society is going through radically transformative periods, which has happened more than once throughout history. It is typical of those times that the basic beliefs and assumptions about the nature of the universe, humanity's place in it, and the existence and relevance of divine beings are questioned, debated, and revised, if not always improved. One can see that this is true simply by studying what was happening in the Western Hemisphere prior to and during the sixteenth century Protestant Reformation (focused on God's accessibility) and the eighteenth century Enlightenment (focused on God's relevance). The questions and issues being asked and raised today are not noticeably different from those that were asked and raised multiple times centuries ago. The modern Western world clearly demonstrates its arrogance in the proud but unsupportable claim that it has reached heights unattained by prior civilizations. This may be true in the technological realm, but not in religious and philosophical realms. As someone put it centuries ago, "What has been is what will be, and what has been done is what will be done; there is nothing new under the sun."[2] The 1960s were not unique except perhaps in one regard: the decade saw both the rise of the death of God theology and the banning of prayer and Bible reading in public schools, as a result of a hard-fought campaign

2. Eccl 1:9.

by proudly self-avowed atheist Madalyn Murray O'Hare. In *Murray v. Curlett* the U.S. Supreme Court ruled that publicly funded schools could not require students to participate in religious activities because it violated the Free Exercise and Establishment Clauses of the U.S. Constitution. It was an exercise in futility; O'Hare is dead, the sad victim of a brutal murderer who coveted her money, and students still pray in public schools, albeit not as a school-sponsored activity. One can be sure that some of them still fervently turn to heaven for help passing a test for which they failed to study.

Efforts to curb or curtail religious influence in the larger society have been around for a long time, ebbing and flowing for various reasons. But they gained traction in the 1960s as much of what had long been held sacred and inviolable was called into question. It did not help on the religious front that implementation of the changes called for by the Second Vatican Council of the Roman Catholic Church (1962–1965) was fomenting discontent among the members of an institution that had remained largely unchanged for almost four centuries. This, along with the rise of social, biblical and theological liberalism in some mainline Protestant denominations, pushed people to the fringes of religious involvement and opened the door to philosophies and movements that critically questioned the need for, and validity of, biblical truth, religious belief, and doctrinal positions. Ideas about what constituted true worship began to change, not always in ways people found positive. Attention began shifting from traditional expressions of adoration and praise directed toward God to forms and styles designed primarily to satisfy people's desire for entertainment. This kind of worship tends to make God just another prop in the quest for spiritual self-fulfillment. God is dead in far too many worship services even as his name is invoked, and his blessing sought. Many of the songs used in these services are vacuous, self-centered exercises in repetitive phrasing and simplistic statements about how much we love God—even as we ignore what he wants us to do. We have killed God in these places by removing every sense of transcendent holiness—worship has become an action directed at God instead of a transformative experience of God's holy and awesome presence.

Can we bring God back from the dead in our worship? It depends on how you define worship. One basic definition of worship is deep devotion to someone or something. Given this definition worship has many possible forms, both religious and secular. Deep devotion to one's own wants and desires is self-worship. People worship sports teams and athletes, celebrities, materialism, and knowledge, among others (hero worship). We worship what we believe will bring fulfillment and meaning to our lives (success worship). Even atheists engage in worship. Worship as an act does not require the object of worship to be divine. Worship has become an act of religious onanism in many churches. The way to bring God back to life in our worship is to direct our focus away from ourselves and what we want to God and what he deserves. So long as worship is primarily about satisfying the crowd or attempting to engineer a "conversation with God," it will never truly be what it is intended to be—a life-changing encounter with a transcendent and transforming God.

Most of the conversations about worship I have had centered around purpose, audience, and mechanics. These discussions can be helpful, but they generally focus more on the subject than the object of worship. This is where conversations with atheists can be helpful. Atheists assert that religionists worship nothing at all, which cracks me up because atheism requires as much faith as does belief in a divine being or beings since the existence of gods can neither be proven nor disproven. Instead of denying it or arguing with it, ask yourself on a personal level how true it might be for you. This does not mean that I believe atheists are correct in their assertion that divine beings do not exist. Instead it is an attempt to get at who or what we believe our focus is when we worship. By the way, I do not have a problem with atheists. In fact, I believe they have much to teach people of faith if we will but stop to listen to what they have to say and try to determine why they are saying it. This takes courage, which is why so many opponents of atheism prefer to criticize and attack it rather than intelligently engaging with it. I respect the fact that atheists are honest in their skepticism. They refuse to believe in the existence of divine beings and order their lives accordingly. This is far better than the hypocrisy of those who claim to believe in God but refuse to acknowledge by their words and actions that God has any real influence on their lives. Atheists believe that God never lived. Many institutional Christians function as if God is dead, or at least irrelevant to daily life.

> Owners of dogs will have noticed that, if you provide them with food and water and shelter and affection, they will think you are god. Whereas owners of cats are compelled to realize that, if you provide them with food and water and shelter and affection, they draw the conclusion that they are God.
>
> —CHRISTOPHER HITCHENS[3]

There are those who claim that atheism is a modern phenomenon and the natural result of increasing scientific knowledge and awareness. This is nonsense if for no other reason than that there have always been skeptics who question or deny the existence of divine beings. One major difference between ancient and modern times is that while in modern times the

3. https://www.brainyquote.com/quotes/christopher_hitchens_472423.

line between religion and philosophy is often indecipherably blurred, the ancient Greeks made a clear distinction between philosophical questions about the nature and existence of divine and theological matters having to do with religious worship. Philosophy concerned itself with determining whether divine beings existed but did not deny or denigrate the value of religion. Religion began with the assumption that divine beings exist and then focused its energy of issues of relationship and behavior. We may define it as hypocrisy today, but in the ancient world one could philosophically debate the existence of divine beings while enthusiastically participating in religious rituals. After all, the prevailing opinion was that the gods were real, and no one could be certain that they were not, so it was better to be safe than sorry. One could choose to publicly participate in religious rituals while at the same time privately doubting and even debating the existence of the divine subjects of those rituals. Although I have no way of proving it empirically, I suspect that many Christians have done the same over the centuries, especially in the 1940s and 1950s when religious involvement in America was considered a social obligation, one that did not place undue burdens on participants. These days we call it "lip service" and tolerate it even as we tactfully denounce it because, after all, we do not want people to get upset and leave the church, thereby depriving the institution of whatever contributions they may be making. Churches that exist solely to please people may flourish for a time, but they are doomed to die because they cannot indefinitely offer the commitment-free pleasures the world offers.

Worship in the religious realm is ideally a ritual act designed to draw the sincere participant into a meaningful interaction with the divine. Catholic churches in both the East and the West are generally much better at this than mainline Protestants. I had a conversation recently that brought this home for me. All the Presbyterian churches in which I have participated or helped lead had an unwritten but often stated expectation that the worship service should last no more than an hour, frequently for reasons having to do mostly with personal convenience. To be fair, sometimes this expectation was built on the practical fact that there were multiple services and time was needed for volunteers to set up and prepare for the next service or because educational opportunities for children coincided with one or more of the services and volunteers expected to start and finish at certain times. Pastors rail against time restrictions (I was once in their camp), since in their opinion it is not right to limit the worship of God to a single hour when people are willing to spend hours attending events that have nothing to do with God or religion. This assertion was forcibly presented to me after I had the audacity to suggest than an hour-long service was enough. The problem is that at least half of the time people spend in church during the average Protestant worship service of any length involves not active worship but passive listening. It is not so much that pastors want more time for people to worship as it is that they want more time to preach, some of them being convinced that the wisdom they want to share from the pulpit will change the church and move it in a positive direction. The reality is that most people forget what the pastor said as soon as the final "amen" is pronounced, if not sooner. People may get a spiritual high during an inspiring message or uplifting service, but true, lasting spiritual growth does not happen in worship. Most pastors may not believe that God is dead, but they rarely have a problem taking God's place as the object of worship for most of the service.

> For God to prove himself on demand, physically, would be a grave disappointment, and the strongest Christians should be considerably grateful that he chooses not to do so. The skeptic endlessly demands proof, yet God refuses to insult the true intelligence of man, the '6th sense', the chief quality, the acumen which distinguishes man from the rest of creation, faith.
>
> —CRISS JAMI[4]

The impulse to believe in something larger than ourselves is hardwired into the human consciousness, which is why the pertinent question must constantly be asked: Do divine beings exist? Moderns in the West often act as if questions related to the existence of a god or gods are vital matters of life and death for all humanity. Perhaps they are, but the reality is that what one believes is a personal matter. You are free to declare that God is dead. You are free to accept or deny the existence of divine being(s). Despite what some religions and denominations claim, you are free to believe or deny any and every assertion made by every religion or philosophy. You are free to choose how you want to live and what you want to believe. You are not, however, free to determine the consequences of your choices. You may evade them for a time, but there is one instance in which avoidance is impossible: Personal choice does not determine what happens to you after you die, except perhaps regarding your funeral arrangements and the final disposition of your body. Even then, you cannot reliably ensure that your wishes will be respected. You cannot choose what happens to you after you die, but you can make choices that give you at least a measure of assurance regarding your eternal destiny. The real issue is, having made a choice in the matter of eternity, what are you going to do about it? The answer varies from religion to religion and philosophy to philosophy and can be simple,

4. https://www.azquotes.com/author/52468-Criss_Jami/tag/atheist.

complex, or somewhere in the middle. If you identify as a follower of Jesus, the answer, in my opinion, is simple: Obey his commands, put your hope in him for eternal life, and tell others about him. Please note that this does not include browbeating, lecturing, nagging, or forcibly compelling people to believe in Jesus or in some bizarre doctrine about him "for salvation." This was never part of the mission, at least according to the words of Jesus. He clearly told his followers to powerfully proclaim and peacefully persuade people to accept his invitation of a loving relationship with his heavenly Father through him, not to coerce or compel belief. Let the message speak for itself and allow belief to arise from within rather than trying to impose it from without.

> Whenever you enter a town and its people welcome you, eat what is set before you; cure the sick who are there, and say to them, 'The kingdom of God has come near to you.' But whenever you enter a town and they do not welcome you, go out into its streets and say, 'Even the dust of your town that clings to our feet, we wipe off in protest against you. Yet know this: the kingdom of God has come near.'

> —JESUS OF NAZARETH[5]

The account of his earthly life and ministry referenced above reports that when Jesus sent seventy of his followers out ahead of him to prepare towns for his arrival he told them to stay where they were welcomed and peacefully leave any community that did not want them or their message. (Refer to the previous section if you have forgotten the content.) Jesus did not tell them to stay and argue with those who disagreed, nor did he give them permission to coerce belief. This well-documented evangelistic approach of the first few generations of Jesus followers seems to have focused far more on relationship than gaining assent to a specific set of doctrinal assertions. Their faith, and the proclamation of their faith remained the same even in the face of rejection and persecution by family and friends. That changed when an influential Christian in Caesarea (northern Palestine) named Eusebius was in the right place at the right time to achieve official state recognition of his version of Christian doctrine, one that was rejected by a vocal minority of Christians. His beliefs were closer to the first generation of Jesus' followers than those of Christians based in Europe, but the means he used to win the day were not laudable. A theological debate became a political war and what followed was a decades-long struggle between the two largest theological divisions to secure the dubious power to

5. Luke 10:8–11.

politically enforce and impose its doctrinal assertions about the natures of God and Jesus on all Christians. God took a back seat to doctrine, and chaos reigned in Christian churches around the world.

It was not a laudable time in the history of institutional Christianity. The fierce debates that raged across the Roman Empire (ruled by then from Constantinople, not Rome), beginning in 325 AD, were addressed in church councils in various locations over several centuries, but no view prevailed as the accepted truth except the official conciliar pronouncements, adherence to which was enforced by the state. Theological positions were deeply held in those days even among the common people. This may have helped create an environment in which the losing side chose not to convert to the views of the majority even when faced with the threat of arrest, imprisonment, torture, and death; instead, it went underground where it continued to gain followers. (There has always been something compelling about rooting for the underdog.) Doctrinal and theological differences among Christians in the Roman Empire might have remained relatively peaceful matters of academic debate, but instead they were exacerbated by political and cultural divisions and resulted in a schism between Eastern and Western Catholicism about a millennium ago, one that tragically exists to the present day. It is tragic in my view because although some in the West will argue the point, much of what the church in the East declares as true predates the doctrines promulgated in the West. Dead doctrines took the place of a living God, paving the way, in my opinion, for the birth and spread of Islam.

Attempts to impose a specific set of beliefs and doctrines on adherents as a condition of eternal salvation have never been very effective. This has been true for a long time, even as far back as the days of Moses. It seems that even as the Law was being delivered to the people, the expectation was that they would rapidly and continually disobey it.[6] Faithfulness was encouraged (some would say coerced) by the linking of obedience to reward and disobedience to punishment, but the expectation was that people were able to make the right choice even if it was a struggle to do so. Institutional Christianities from the most conservative to the most liberal still try to impose a specific set of beliefs and practices on their adherents, ones that directly oppose each other, which is a problem when one's eternal destiny becomes contingent upon accepting the right set of doctrines. The most obvious examples are sexuality and gender issues. One side says that anyone who claims to be homosexual, transgendered, non-gendered, or

6. "For I know that after my death you are sure to become utterly corrupt and to turn from the way I have commanded you. In days to come, disaster will fall on you because you will do evil in the sight of the LORD and arouse his anger by what your hands have made" (Deut 31:29, NIV).

any other kind of gendered is bound for hell. The other side says that not only are these people going to heaven but that anyone who disagrees with their gender choice is bound for hell. Both sides claim to be holding the correct Christian position. Both sides are wrong. Going or not going to heaven has nothing to do with gender, sexuality, politics, theology, or any other type of human criteria. Christianity, if it is to be true to its founder, neither condemns nor condones, seeking instead to help people find ultimate fulfillment in someone other than themselves. Any attempt to coerce any kind of belief or behavior in the context of religious faith and practice is doomed to fail, especially when they have little or no relation to faith and religious practice.

> My point is, however, that churches do promote beliefs that would more appropriately find a place in a context of intellectual debate. They wind up cheerleading for highly dubious opinions on historical, scientific, and metaphysical matters, simply on the bases of emotional preference and the inertia of tradition. They demand conformity to these beliefs, and if you cannot swim with the current, then, well partner, maybe you'd be happier in another pool, another lake in fact, the one ablaze with burning sulfur.
>
> —ROBERT M. PRICE[7]

Because they are human constructs, institutions typically demand adherence to a common set of beliefs, values and practices. This is one way they ensure their survival. Successful institutions, at least according to worldly standards, create a culture of conformity, one that often impacts the lives of employees outside the walls of the institution. If you are part of such a culture, ask yourself how often you are expected to take work home or be on call at all hours of the day and night, even when you are supposedly on vacation. Some institutions can inspire this kind of behavior by cultivating a sense of loyalty and devotion through flexible hours, bonuses, rewards, and other perks. Other institutions seek to coerce it through threats of punishment, lost wages, and termination, or by cynically giving their employees the sense that they are indispensable to the growth and success of the company. Institutional Christianities in modern times most often use tactics related to the former rather than the latter, but historically the latter has been well used. It was possible for the institution to coerce certain kinds of behavior when religious belief was an integral part of the fabric of society and threats of eternal damnation were taken seriously. Such is rarely the case today in

---

7. https://www.azquotes.com/author/23722-Robert_M_Price.

the institutional Christianities of the Western world. The diminishing levels of religious belief and church attendance today show that coercion no longer works and that there is little sense of loyalty to any individual church or religions institution. This is yet another proof for the death of God in the heart of institutional Christianity. Dead doctrines do not inspire vibrant faith; only a living God can instill a living faith in people.

Churches that claim to have a lock on ultimate truth are failing because people refuse to be coerced into believing that anything of a spiritual nature is absolute. Churches that claim no one has a lock on the truth and that everyone is right do not have anything compelling to offer to those with quick and easy access to an overabundance of educational and entertainment options. This is one reason why institutional Christianities across the Western world are becoming increasingly irrelevant and dying. Old historic buildings and new state-of-the-art campuses are becoming mausoleums dedicated to dead religions full of spiritually dead people worshipping dead gods of their own creation. Visit an empty church building during the week (most of them are) and you will easily sense what I mean. A church building that sits mostly empty except on Sunday and a few evenings a week is wasted space and a drain on resources that would be better utilized to help the hurting and bring hope to the hopeless. Institutional Christianities will never be truly faithful to the mission Jesus gave to the church until and unless they are spending far more money on ministry than they are on salaries, buildings, and programs.

Why does any of this matter? The answer is as subjective as the question. If you identify as a religious or spiritual person, or are just curious about such matters, then you may find what follows interesting. The reason this matters from my perspective is because eternity is at stake. It *is* a matter of life and death. Those who believe that death is followed by oblivion have little reason to care about the desires or commands of divine beings whose existence cannot be proven empirically. Those who hope for life after death have reason to be concerned. Regardless of their religious beliefs, what matters most is how the way one acts and what one believes impacts one's eternal disposition. As much as we might like to delude ourselves otherwise, we have no control over our eternal destiny and neither does any other mere mortal. We do not get to decide. Universalism, which has much to recommend it otherwise, asserts that one's eternal destiny is a matter of choice. This is nonsense. They apparently believe that it is really is simply a matter of choosing whether you want to spend eternity in the smoking or the non-smoking section. If this *is* true, then every religion is irrelevant, which is, of course, what many atheists claim.

> "Where has God gone?" he cried. "I shall tell you. We have killed him—you and I. We are his murderers."
>
> —FRIEDRICH NIETZSCHE[8]

If you have stayed with me this far, I am going to assume that you want to carry this to the next level. The next question is: "Where is God?" In its proper context, it is not a spatial question but a philosophical one, which makes sense given that the first modern occurrence of this question appeared in the German philosopher Friedrich Nietzsche's book *The Gay Science* (1882). He repeated it in the works that poured forth from his pen during a frenetic decade of writing prior to his mental collapse in 1889 at the age of forty-four. Taken in its proper context, the question is an expression of the idea that the Enlightenment put to death any possibility of belief in God. The *Time* magazine article referenced at the beginning of this chapter mentions Nietzsche and this statement. It was a timely inclusion (pardon the pun) given the turmoil taking place in and around most of the institutional Christianities in the Western world then.[9] The Second Vatican Council had recently closed[10], bringing with it changes that many Catholics used as an excuse to stop attending Mass, even as they continued to identify as Roman Catholic. Large segments of Protestantism were increasingly focused on social justice and political activism at the expense of traditional beliefs and values, based on political and social movements, which redefined their reading, interpretation, and preaching of the Bible. The superficial veneer of institutional religion was beginning to show signs of wear even as it clung tenaciously to its social position. Although 97 percent of Americans claimed to believe in God in 1966, only 27 percent claimed that their beliefs were deeply held. God was quickly taking a back seat to other issues that were deemed more important than simply believing, trusting, and obeying.

The issue in 1966, as timely today as it was then, is whether faith in divine beings is still relevant. Does religion matter in the modern world? Many people identify as "spiritual but not religious," whatever that means. Divine beings may exist, but does humanity need them in any sense of the word? The answer is, of course, debatable. Humanity has always been drawn toward belief in the divine in whatever form that may take, as may perhaps be proven by the existence of religious artifacts from nearly every era of human existence. Some will accept this as fact, others will not, but if we allow

---

8. "Nietzsche" as follows: https://www.goodreads.com/quotes/406593-where-has-god-gone-the-madman-asked-i-shall-tell

9. I hold to a broad definition of Christianity: If a movement places Jesus at its center and points to him as the means of entering eternal life, then it is Christian.

10. Pope Paul VI closed it on December 8, 1965.

for the existence of a god or gods, then the more pressing question is the continuing legitimacy of the institutions that claim responsibility for regulating and defining what it means to believe in, worship, and serve divine beings as conceived in the minds of those who choose to acknowledge their existence and influence on the world. Institutional Christianities attempt to define and regulate faith, but all they can do is regulate doctrine and practice. Doctrines are human attempts to explain matters of faith using various proofs, mostly from the Bible. Faith is belief in the existence of beings without any empirical proof and without dependence on the Bible. The Bible was never intended to be the only source of faith in God. Instead, the Bible assumes that the one reading it wants to learn about God and has felt at least a flicker of faith prior to doing so. Not everyone reads the Bible this way, of course. Some read it selectively looking for evidence to disprove or discredit it, often finding what they want to find by reading it without faith.

The sad reality is that God *is* dead, or at least terminally ill. I do not mean that in an ontological sense; I have no claim to special revelatory knowledge about the effectual status of define beings. My point, like Nietzsche, is that God is dead or dying in the hearts of many people in the world today, and especially in institutional religious bodies in the Western Hemisphere that claim to have a lock on what it means to believe in God/Elohim/Allah or whatever term they judge most appropriate to refer to deity. I know a little about Islam, more about Judaism, and the most about Christianity in its Western forms, both Catholic and Protestant. Islam and Judaism have their share of problems, none of which I am qualified to address. Hence my focus on Western institutional Christianity, often referred to as the Church. The boundary between institutional Christianity and the Church is porous. Some institutional expressions of Christianity retain elements of an organic faith. At the same time, there are organic expressions of Christianity that reject institutionalism in any form. There is an important distinction to be made between the Church as a living organism, which is how Jesus and the first generation of his followers defined it, and the Church as an institutional construct, which is what it became far earlier in its existence than many are willing to admit. The former will live until the end of human history; the latter will die, as it has died in many times and many places throughout history, to be replaced by something that will endure for a time but will also be replaced.

People make lots of noise about how religion is no longer relevant, and that humanity will be better off when we dispense with superstitious belief in beings that claim the authority to tell us how to act. Although their motives may be questioned, their point is valid. Religions, insofar as they are human-built institutions, rise and fall with the whims of preference, politics, and cultural persuasion. The primary issue is not so much the effectiveness of institutional religion as it is the relationship between established religion and faith. People of faith form institutions as a way of banding together around a common set of beliefs and supporting one another as they strive to live out what they believe. Institutions may start with pure intentions but ultimately give into the urge to place survival of the institution above any other concern. This has happened time and again in the history of Christianity. Periodic efforts are made to curb the most egregious institutional abuses, but the ones that have advocated the most radical changes were persecuted out of existence, often in the name of Christ, or quickly found themselves on the periphery, universally opposed by institutional bureaucrats of all stripes who might otherwise be sworn enemies. It has been said that the first step in effecting a cure is admitting that there is a problem. If this is true, then we need to admit that God is dead in the heart of institutional Christianity and move forward from there, beginning with those in every position of leadership.

> Most churches do not grow beyond the spiritual health of their leadership. Many churches have a pastor who is trying to lead people to a Savior he has yet to personally encounter. If spiritual gifting is no proof of authentic faith, then certainly a job title isn't either.
>
> —Darrin Patrick[11]

The harsh truth is that God is dead not only in the lives of people who are quick to claim otherwise, but also in the hearts of far too many church leaders who claim to selflessly serve him but who really want little more than a position of power from which to lord it over others. They cajole the faithful into making financial sacrifices while simultaneously seeking justification for their own self-centered, decadent lifestyles. Institutional Christianities in the West provide them the opportunities to accomplish these goals, but only if they start out in the best churches and study at a flagship seminary where they shamelessly cultivate relationships with the most renowned professors to facilitate their ability to secure positions in the largest, most theologically correct churches. The trend in all but a few of the largest of these churches is to try to maintain a façade of traditionalism while simultaneously installing state-of-the-art projection and sounds systems costing tens of thousands of dollars, covering up stained glass windows and artwork with screens, filling the front of the church with instruments of all kinds, and dumbing down the gospel message to appeal to the lowest common denominator. The impulse is to "throw the baby out with

---

11. https://www.goodreads.com/author/quotes/3430631.Darrin_Patrick.

the bathwater" and dispense with every doctrine, belief, custom, practice, or worship style that non-believers might find unacceptable without stopping to consider how such wholesale denigration of tradition will impact those who are in the best position to make a positive Christian impact in the community. This is the inevitable result of the church compromising itself to the values, beliefs, and priorities of a world that openly hates and opposes nearly everything challenging about Jesus and his message.

Institutional Christianities in the West are narcissistic behemoths slowly starving to death for lack of meaningful attention. There are individual congregations striving to do good and be faithful, but they are often being pushed to the fringes by one form of institutionalism or another. So-called "independent" churches, especially the largest ones, are just as prone to the disease of institutionalism because many of them adopt institutional structures and practices that focus more on the growth of networks, programs, and membership than on spiritual nurture and growth, all protests to the contrary. The best way to describe the state of the institutional church in the West is as a macabre creature carefully assembled of disparate, mismatched pieces by a mad scientist in a secluded lab. In short, the institutional Christianities of the Western world are akin to the poor creature assembled by Dr. Frankenstein and unintentionally sent out to bring horror and terror to the world. There was good in the creature, but its outward appearance rendered that good incapable of accomplishing anything and ultimately resulted in tragedy. The same can reasonably be said to be true for institutional Christianity.

Chapter 4

Shed No Tears for Frankenstein's Monster

> "Hateful day when I received life!" I exclaimed in agony.
> "Accursed creator! Why did you form a monster so hideous that
> even you turned from me in disgust? God, in pity, made man
> beautiful and alluring, after his own image; but my form is a filthy
> type of yours, more horrid even from the very resemblance."
>
> —THE MONSTER, MARY SHELLEY, *FRANKENSTEIN*[1]

The story of Frankenstein's monster as Mary Wollstonecraft Shelley originally wrote it is far different from the cinematic versions produced over the years. Shelly chose not to describe the creature's manufacture or its appearance in detail. While we are given the distinct impression that it was assembled using parts from dead bodies, the only facts we learn about its appearance is that it was male, eight feet tall, had skin that was a deathly yellowish cast, and was immensely strong and agile. It was also highly intelligent and articulate, its brain having been undamaged in the process of its creation. The monster was initially persecuted because of its appearance, not its actions, by those few people it encountered. Aside from some petty thefts, the crimes it committed were designed to bring misery into the life of its creator. In contrast, many, though not all, of the popular movies portray the monster as little more than an animal driven by the urge to destroy everyone and everything in its path. This raises a question: When is a monster truly a monster? I find it interesting that Shelley's book was published in London in 1818, some four decades before the birth of a "monster" in Leicester, United

1. https://www.goodreads.com/quotes/293371-hateful-day-when-i-received-life-i-exclaimed-in-agony

Kingdom named Joseph Merrick, better known to the world as the Elephant Man. I wonder if Merrick would have been treated better if people had read and taken to heart Shelley's message. Is it better to fear the monster and seek its destruction, or to pity it and try to help? The question is relevant.

What would Jesus think of the "monster" that calls itself "the church" and calls him as its creator? Although I cannot claim any special revelation, I suspect that he would take one look at the misshapen creature we have cobbled together in his name, turn away in disgust, and declare with force, "I never knew you."[2] Then he would gather together those who have faithfully walked in his footsteps according to his way of life and leave the institution to die in whatever way seems best to it. It is nothing short of a miracle that Christianity—often equated in popular culture with charlatans in fancy suits parading around in front of huge audiences of adoring fans declaring that God's only desire is to make their lives comfortable—has managed to produce people, typically from the least influential strata of society, whose simple faith spread the light and love of Jesus across the world. This, despite an institution that persecuted them, in some cases hounding them to their deaths, and occasionally venerating them as saints afterwards—all in the name of Christ! There is no excuse for Christians persecuting other Christians, yet this has been done in the past and is shamefully still being done today.

Before you find fault with this assessment, take a moment to consider carefully how you view Christians with whom you disagree or refuse to acknowledge as Christian because their beliefs differ from your own.[3] Even universalists and, increasingly, progressives are guilty of this, in that the only universal truth they are willing to acknowledge is that there is no universal truth. All over the world there are Protestants who hate Catholics, Catholics who hate Protestants, Protestants who hate other Protestants, and Catholics who hate other Catholics. It sometimes seems like everyone hates the Mormons and the Jehovah's Witness, and there are members of both groups who eagerly return the favor. This is ironic given that nearly every group of Christians has been through a period of persecution, which you would think would make them unwilling to persecute others. Unfortunately, the opposite has almost always been the case. The early church was a persecuted church that quickly, and without any apparent sense of hypocrisy or irony, became a persecutor once it was freed from persecution. Examples abound in the historical record. Arians and Nestorians in

---

2. Concerning those who mistakenly believed that serving their own idea of what it means to follow Jesus, seeking only their own aggrandizement, Jesus declared: "And then will I declare to them, 'I never knew you; depart from me, you workers of lawlessness.'" (Matt 7:23, ESV).

3. For instance, Mormons and Jehovah's Witnesses.

the early days, and Anabaptists and Mormons in more recent times, were all hounded, persecuted, tortured, and executed by people claiming to be the true followers of Jesus and, worse, to be acting in his name. How sad it is that religious persecution among "Christians" is still taking place today, albeit with (thankfully) far less physical violence.

> Polluted by crimes, and torn by the bitterest remorse, where can I find rest but in death?
>
> —THE MONSTER, MARY SHELLEY, *FRANKENSTEIN*[4]

If Jesus did not die to bring an institutional religion to life, then the next question is obvious: What *did* Jesus intend to happen after he left his followers to carry on his mission? The most basic answer is that he wanted them to physically and dynamically carry his message to the world, not build a static religious structure to which people were expected to come. The earliest proclamation of the gospel is clear and compelling: Eternal salvation comes through a person not a program; it is about a message, not a monument, about dying to self, not dying for a doctrine. The gospel message is simply this: "God has come near in the person of Jesus. Are you ready to meet him?" To their credit, many of Jesus' followers have been sharing that message with varying degrees of success ever since. Tragically, the message began losing clarity when the movement became the official religious institution of the most powerful empire in the world soon after 325 AD. Was this what Jesus intended for the church? That may seem like a heretical question, and perhaps it is (heresy is subjective and usually determined by those who have the power to enforce their view—ask the Arians or the Anabaptists), but it is fundamental to what follows.

Institutional Christianity has done much, intentionally or not, to foster ignorance among the faithful, often as an attempt to maintain control over them. It has cobbled together rules and regulations ostensibly designed to help the faithful grow spiritually, but which were sometimes crafted to enrich the institution and expand its power. For example, at various times and for a variety of reasons, the institutional church prohibited its members from reading the Bible in any language except Latin, and even discouraged them from reading the Bible at all. The institution reserved for itself the right to interpret Scripture and determine doctrine. The church emphasized whatever supported its claims to complete control over every aspect of life and death, at least of the common people. They were particularly keen, at least by the fourth century, to distance Christianity as far as possible from its Jewish roots for reasons that had more to do with bigotry, jealousy, and

---

4. https://www.goodreads.com/quotes/411688-polluted-by-crimes-and-torn-by-the-bitterest-remorse-where

greed than anything else. The mistaken beliefs that resulted from this are still around today. Did you know that some people sincerely believe that Jesus was the first Christian? This is nonsense given that a Christian is, by definition, a follower of Christ (i.e., Jesus). Jesus was God follower not a Jesus follower. The Bible never puts the word "Christian" on the lips of Jesus. This may come as a shock to some, but Jesus also never called his followers Christians. The word "Christ" in Greek means "Messiah" or "Anointed One." It is a title, not a name; Jesus is *the* Christ, i.e., the Savior. It came into use well after the time of Jesus, albeit still within the first generation.

Please note that Jesus did not encourage his followers to abandon their Jewish faith or heritage (although he laid the groundwork for the day when the temple would be destroyed, and the rituals no longer performed). Jesus was a faithful Jew. He believed in God as revealed in the Bible of his people (What Christians regrettably refer to as the "Old" Testament.[5]) Instead of looking at Jesus through the lens of doctrines and beliefs developed long after his time on earth, we need try to get back to the religious culture in which he talked, taught, lived, and walked. It was a time when, although they might revere Jesus as a holy man, no Jew in his or her right mind would have believed he was God in any way, shape, or form. Such a belief was completely inconsistent with Jewish doctrine. Jesus' claim to special status, which bore little difference from claims made by prophets, priests, and kings in Israel's past, was interpreted by his enemies as claims to equality with God, not claims to be God. Yet, it was not these claims for which he was ultimately handed over to the Romans. Instead, it seems to have been his (misunderstood) claim that he would destroy the temple.[6] Thus, does institutional religion ever and always care more for its buildings than its beliefs. The same, unfortunately, is true today. The "temple" of institutional Christianity will be destroyed. What, if anything, will rise in its place?

Jesus participated in the rituals of the institution, but his focus was not on the ongoing survival of the institution. The Jerusalem temple that stood at the ritual heart of Judaism in his day had been under construction for about five decades when Jesus walked the earth and would not be completed for another thirty. It was built on the foundations of a humble temple (finished in 516 BC) that replaced splendid edifice constructed in the time of Solomon and destroyed by the Babylonians in 586 BC. Herod's magnificent temple, said to rival that of Solomon, did not long survive its

---

5. It is more properly titled the "Hebrew Scriptures." My seminary professors would be proud.

6. But they did not find any, though many false witnesses came forward. Finally, two came forward and declared, "This fellow said, 'I am able to destroy the temple of God and rebuild it in three days.'" (Matt 26:60–61, NIV).

completion; it was destroyed in AD 70 by Roman legions under command of Titus, who became emperor of Rome in AD 79. Jerusalem and the temple were not destroyed for religious reasons, at least from the perspective of Rome. It was a political response to the Jewish rebellion that began in AD 66 and was not fully suppressed until AD 136 during what is now known as the Bar Kokhba revolt. All this is to say that Jesus did not see a viable future for religious faith in human institutions and buildings. It is worth noting that both what was known as "Second Temple Judaism" and what can best be called "Jewish Christianity" perished in AD 70 as Jews and Christians alike were dispersed from Jerusalem and forced to redefine their religious and communal existence. It started out well enough, but expansion into the world outside the confines of Palestine was fraught with peril.

> I ought to be thy Adam, but I am rather the fallen angel . . .
>
> —The Monster, Mary Shelley, *Frankenstein*[7]

What happened to the followers of Jesus when they left the confines of Jerusalem and ventured out into the Roman Empire? One of the first things they realized is that they were quickly becoming a minority in their own movement. Non-Jews were swelling the ranks of what was beginning to be called Christianity.[8] Few truly understood the Jewish roots of their new faith. Many tried to merge their new beliefs with their philosophical understandings, resulting in a plethora of different views about the nature of Jesus and his relationship to the God he called his heavenly Father. It is interesting to note that the early church was far more concerned with behavior than doctrine. The gospel message was that there were no distinctions of class, race, or gender in the divine kingdom that Jesus brought into being. This was a radical notion in a culture that defined itself by and was ordered according to its societal divisions. The gospel message was aimed at establishing a family of faith without internal distinctions, not disseminating a new doctrine about a divine or semi-divine being. Almost three hundred years passed before the leaders within what might be loosely referred to as Christianity decided it would be a good idea to establish once and for all a definitive statement about the nature of Jesus apart from his ministry and message. This was the moment at which the parts of the monster that would become institutional Christianity began to be unwittingly assembled by

---

7. https://www.goodreads.com/quotes/48623-how-dangerous-is-the-acquirement-of-knowledge-and-how-much

8. "and when he found him, he brought him to Antioch. So for a whole year Barnabas and Saul met with the church and taught great numbers of people. The disciples were called Christians first at Antioch" (Acts 11:26, NIV).

people who believed they were making something strong, good, and beautiful. In their quest to make the simple message of a Jewish rabbi palatable to a Greek world, they sought to reframe it using terms that properly belonged to philosophy. Knowledge is good, but not if it becomes the object of our worship. Then it becomes a monster, one that will devour us all.

> "How dangerous is the acquirement of knowledge and how much happier that man is who believes his native town to be the world, than he who aspires to be greater than his nature will allow."
>
> —VICTOR FRANKENSTEIN TO THE MONSTER,
> MARY SHELLEY, *FRANKENSTEIN*[9]

The endeavor to transform Christianity into a philosophical movement began in earnest in the fourth century. More than two centuries passed during which Christians fought long and hard over the nature of Jesus and his relationship to the Father and the Spirit. No proposed doctrine satisfied everyone. What ultimately resulted was the creation of a species of Frankenstein's monster: doctrines cobbled together over the decades that resulted in opposing collections of statements, many of which were incomprehensible to anyone without an advanced understanding of philosophy and a knowledge of both Greek and Latin. This would be all well and good if not for the fact that assent to these doctrines was enforced at the point of a sword. Chief among them was the assertion that Jesus the Christ and God the Father were one and the same. This was "proven" by recourse to philosophical words and concepts that do not appear in the Bible. Anyone who dared to argue that Jesus could not both "be God" and be "sent from God" was told to be quiet and accept it on faith as an incomprehensible mystery, one that was necessary for salvation. The problem with this is that Jesus came to simplify faith, not to complicate it. It is well within the realm of Jewish belief and history for Jesus to be a man chosen by God, adopted as his son, imbued with the Spirit, and ordained for a special purpose without making him God or even equal to God. This is what happens whenever the attempt is made to graft a dead philosophy onto a living faith. The same thing is happening in the Western world today. It is also still true today that doctrines do not save; Jesus saves.

Did Jesus expect his followers to believe that he was God in the flesh? I believe that they would have rejected it out of hand. To be fair, the early church was clearly not united in how it understood Jesus. It allowed for diverse opinions about his nature for almost three centuries if for no other reason than it was facing the more pressing issue of surviving in a

---

9. https://www.goodreads.com/quotes/224643-i-ought-to-be-thy-adam-but-i-am-rather

world that was working to destroy it. Nowhere in the Bible do we find a clear, systematic presentation of the doctrines about Jesus to which some Christians cling so desperately today. Early Christian preaching focused on the new age that Jesus inaugurated when he died on the cross and God raised him from the dead—not on his divine/human nature. In fact, the two accounts of Jesus' conception and birth were only written down after believers and non-believers with backgrounds in Greek philosophy began denying that Jesus had been a physical human being who really lived and died The first evangelists spoke of Jesus as the bearer of God's Word for the world and the mediator of the salvation God offers to humanity, not as God. They viewed Jesus, in keeping with their Jewish context, as a human being whom God had set apart and marked as the Messiah by raising him from the dead. He is, to quote the apostle Paul, the "first fruits of those who have died,"[10] which means that his resurrection makes possible the eternal resurrection of all who have faith in him. Even when John declares that "the Word became flesh and made his dwelling among us,"[11] he was talking not about divine conception but divine election, or to use a word fraught with controversy in the history of Christian doctrine, divine adoption. The Word of God is the Spirit of God is the power of God. It is the power with which God imbues those whom he sets aside to accomplish his purposes (like the prophets, for example).

The proclamation of the gospel by the first followers of Jesus did not focus on the nature of Jesus and his relationship to the Father; it began with a simple question and response:

> Q: What must I do to be saved?
> A: Believe on the Lord Jesus.[12]

Note how the answer is framed: "Believe *on* the Lord Jesus." The preposition used here indicates location. The phrase could also be translated "put your faith/trust in Jesus." My point is this: salvation is rooted in a person, not institutions or doctrinal propositions. The Frankenstein's monster analogy applies here. The key to the "monster's" existence was its brain. There is no mention in the original novel of any damage done to the brain, making its new life even more tragic. The monster is depicted as intelligent, but like a newborn baby. It quickly learns what it needs to survive,

10. But Christ has indeed been raised from the dead, the firstfruits of those who have fallen asleep (1 Cor 15:20, NIV).

11. The Word became flesh and made his dwelling among us (John 1:14, NIV).

12. He then brought them out and asked, "Sirs, what must I do to be saved?" They replied, "Believe in the Lord Jesus, and you will be saved—you and your household" (Acts 16:30–31, NIV).

eventually discovering that it is a hideous caricature of a human being, one that its creator intended to be the perfect representation of humanity. Victor Frankenstein may be more successful in this endeavor than he thought. The monster may have been a failed attempt to represent a perfect human, but it is certainly an apt representation of the institutional church.

The "brain" of Christianity—the message of salvation in and through Jesus—remains true today but is hidden in a caricature of the body Jesus intended to house and nurture it. I can state with confidence that not one person is saved by belief in doctrines or sets of theological assertions—there is nothing to that effect in the Bible. Doctrines more often bring death than life, having been responsible for the murders of countless people, if not the outright extermination of entire groups, through the ages. For example, a group known as the Anabaptists were persecuted, tortured, and executed in the sixteenth century by people claiming to be Christians simply because they refused to acknowledge, based on their understanding of the Bible, the validity of infant baptism. (There is no definitive evidence in the Bible to either support or to refute the practice of infant baptism.) It is a non-essential. Jesus does not care. In fact, the first Jesus followers did not care. Every picture of baptism in the Bible shows it happening after a decision of faith is made, not before. Baptism does not save anyone.

What was central for Jesus is central for us: "The time is fulfilled, and the kingdom of God is at hand; repent and believe in the gospel."[13] What is the gospel? The apostle Paul, speaking from his Jewish context, helps us. What was central for Paul is central for us: Jesus was a real human being, really died on a Roman cross, really rose bodily from the dead, really ascended into heaven, is presently seated at the right hand of the Father and will physically come again in the future to judge the world and usher in the kingdom of God. All doctrinal assertions aside, Jesus believed that God had anointed him for a mission that would culminate in his death on a cross after being convicted of a crime he did not commit. He believed God would raise him from the dead. Jesus knew that his life's purpose was to reconcile God and humanity, restoring the harmony God intended for the relationship from the beginning. He spent more time teaching about the nature of this relationship and its impact on humanity than he did on doctrinal pronouncements. Jesus focused on bringing hope to the helpless, hurting, and oppressed, not establishing an institution. His intention, like that of Martin Luther fifteen centuries later, was to reform how people understood how God relates to us, not on creating a new religion.

13. Mark 1:15, ESV.

"If our impulses were confined to hunger, thirst, and desire, we might be nearly free; but now we are moved by every wind that blows and a chance word or scene that that word may convey to us."

—THE MONSTER, MARY SHELLEY, *FRANKENSTEIN*[14]

A key element of Jesus' teaching was that religion, as valuable as it may be, has no power to save. Salvation comes from God, not from human institutions. This allows us to see a picture of the "Frankenstein's Monster" aspect of institutional Christianity. Every expression of Christianity, almost without exception, has cobbled together its own legal code using selected portions of the Torah, statements Jesus made in the Gospels, and social mores current to its time and culture. Each group claims to know which laws are valid and which are cultural prohibitions related to a specific time or situation and therefore no longer valid. All of this is too convenient because it provides dubious justification for setting aside inconvenient laws while allowing us to give into our worst instincts based on the "law of love." If we are willing to trust our Jewish brothers and sisters as we read Jesus' words, we will discover that the laws having to do with how we conduct ourselves relationally, morally, and ethically are still in force; Jesus affirmed them and expanded upon them in his teaching. It is important to understand that obedience is always an expression of faith, not a guarantee of a place in heaven. The danger we face in dismissing the law code of Judaism is that we are then tempted to set aside obedience of any kind as relevant to our faith. We cannot simply claim that inchoate faith in "Jesus" (however we picture or define him) means that we have assurance of eternal life. It is the relationship that saves, not belief in whatever we want Jesus to be for us. And the relationship determines how we live.

I am not suggesting that we need a new institution (God forbid!), nor am I calling for a new reformation in the historical sense of the term. Reformations produce more institutions and ultimately fail to address core problems. Even a cursory examination of the history of religions shows that every reformation movement, no matter how laudable and pure the reasons for starting it, fell to corruption and in-fighting, sooner or later adopting beliefs and practices it sought to change in the first place. No reformed movement long survives the death of those under whose guidance it began. The peaceful and peace-loving Jesus movement, where disputes over matters of belief were settled with (sometimes heated) words, gave way in less than three centuries to an institution made up of at least two, and sometimes three,

14. https://www.goodreads.com/quotes/102225-if-our-impulses-were-confined-to-hunger-thirst-and-desire

competing groups each vying for the support of the monarchs of the day to enforce their point of view by utilizing the state-sanctioned torture and death of their theological opponents. After all, it would not do for "faithful Christians" to get their hands dirty. The many reformations of the church that began with Martin Luther of Germany and Henry VIII of England were just that: reformations, or more accurately, restructurings of an institution, not renewal of a faith. They focused on doctrine and ecclesiastical authority, not bringing the heart of the gospel into the hearts of people. None of them did much to definitively correct the systemic corruptions they sought to remedy. Most reformed movements were as guilty of using force to suppress their enemies as were those who promoted, funded, and promulgated the Crusades and the Spanish Inquisition.

I used to believe that the thousands of different Christian denominations in the world served a useful purpose. Diversity is good, right? Not in this case, but let me explain what I mean. Every new movement or denomination further weakens the cause for which Jesus called people to follow him. One reason for this is that it creates confusion among believers and non-believers alike, and thereby casts doubt on the validity of Christianity in any expression. The earliest communities of Jesus followers were not uniform in their beliefs about some aspects of their faith, but they were all in agreement as to the essentials: Jesus is the Savior of the world who died in atonement for the sins of humanity, whom God raised from the dead—thereby breaking the power of sin and death—and who has opened to door to eternal life to all who will believe in him and receive him as the Lord of their lives. The last part is the most crucial. The first generation of Christians believed salvation was only possible in and through a relationship with Jesus, which was found in community with other Jesus followers, not through membership in an institution.

Every honest historian and scholar will recognize that there has never been any such thing as a monolithic unity called Christianity except in the world of fantasy. There have always been a multitude of Christianities, most of them institutional in some shape or form after Christianity became a state-sponsored religion in the fourth century. This is unfortunate. As I recall, Jesus commanded his followers to make disciples, not institutions. Disciples serve Jesus; institutions demand to be served. Disciples give their lives for Jesus; institutions demand that those who belong to them give and do whatever it takes to preserve the institution. All the jokes notwithstanding, there will be neither churches nor denominations in heaven. Anyone who dies and wakes up in a church building assuredly did not end up in heaven. I say this as one who has spent most of his life in and around churches. I say it not with glee, but with despair. I entered church service in accord with what I believe to be a clear call from Jesus to do so. I had no illusions about growing rich, and every expectation that I would struggle to live up to the call. I naively believed that by going into the ministry I was escaping from the monsters of the world.

The point I want to make is that Jesus called me to serve *him*, not an institution. I still believe this is true. Mystical experiences are not the norm for me. I began my long, strange journey to and through ministry as the result of a compelling dream in which Jesus commanded me to serve him. I took a break from ministry after more than twenty-six years, in part because I felt that I was being pressured to give my life to an institution. No one can reasonably argue that Jesus wants people to place service to a church or a denomination above service to him. To serve Jesus is to answer his call. To serve an institution is idolatry. When religions institutionalize, they become something other than what Jesus intended. The institution almost always becomes more dedicated to its preservation than to carrying out the mission for which it was formed. It becomes a monster, but one to whom little sympathy is due because it chose to become a monster rather than having the condition imposed upon it. This is one reason why I believe that the monster must die. It will die, and I will not long mourn its death. The only hope for the survival of the church is the overt and wide-scale persecution of Christians. This will drive the institution underground where it will survive precisely because it will no longer be an institution.

You may wonder that if I truly believe what I am writing I must believe there is one true church to which every Christian must belong. Wrong. No denomination can claim to be the true church, no matter how much they demand to be acknowledged as such. All of them are flawed and fallible human institutions destined for the dust heap of history. Every denomination formed in opposition to something and is defined not by what it believe, but by what it rejects as untrue. I do not seek the preservation of any denomination or movement. I will shed a tear of sympathy when Frankenstein's monster meets its end, more because of what it could have been than what it became. My only prayer is that what emerges from the broken and bleeding corpse is a faith that is focused on the basics set forth by an itinerant Jewish teacher in a remote part of the world two millennia ago. Monumental changes will need to take place before that prayer is answered, and it is likely that few who are invested in institutional Christianity will approve of them. I have an idea of what will need to happen, and I will share it, but we need to do some more exploring first.

Chapter 5

Beware of Greeks Bearing Gifts

"Going to church doesn't make you a Christian any more than going to a garage makes you an automobile."

—Billy Sunday[1]

Have you ever received a gift or purchased something that you had long anticipated owning only to realize that it was not as wonderful as you thought it would be? You are not alone. I remember Christmases from my childhood when I impatiently waited for the moment when I could tear the wrapping off the package that I knew was going to be *the most amazing present ever*! And it *was* amazing, for an hour. Then it was boring. I suspect that many of us never really grow out of this, especially those who eagerly anticipate the release of the latest gadget or device. The problem is that while these things look good on the outside, they fail to satisfy our built-in desire for lasting fulfillment. Appearances can be deceiving. We know this, but still buy into the advertising hype that surrounds the release of the latest and the best. The "last _____ you will ever need" is never the last one you will ever want. This phenomenon is not new; the tendency to be taken in by outward appearances is as old as humanity.

An example of this is found in the story of the Trojan war, believed to have taken place in the twelfth or thirteenth century BC. According to the *Aeneid* of Virgil, following an unsuccessful ten-year siege of Troy, the Achaeans (Greeks) built a huge wooden horse, hid soldiers inside it, and pretended to sail away. The unsuspecting Trojans took the horse into their city as a victory trophy. The troops hiding inside snuck out after nightfall and opened the gates for the rest of the Achaean army, which had been

1. https://www.brainyquote.com/quotes/billy_sunday_390595.

hiding out of sight, thus ensuring the destruction of Troy.[2] This gave rise to the adage: "Beware of Greeks bearing gifts." Appearances are not always what they seem. These are appropriate adages for this part of our journey.

One of Jesus' most famous followers was, perhaps inadvertently, a Greek bearing gifts, although he would not have defined himself in those terms. There is no middle ground when it comes to an apostle of Jesus named Paul, who by his own admission came late to the game.[3] He did not have an easy go of it. Despite a supernatural conversion experience, something that carried a great deal of weight in those days, the recognized leaders of the Jesus movement headquartered in Jerusalem questioned Paul's apostolic credentials—first because he was not with them during Jesus' earthly ministry, and second because he had publicly and violently opposed them and their mission.[4] Nevertheless, his argument won the day and he tirelessly promoted the Jesus movement in the cities and towns of Asia Minor, a region that was predominantly Greek in culture. His influence on the development and growth of what became institutional Christianity cannot be discounted. Paul's aim appears to have been to promote open membership in Judaism to people who had previously been denied the possibility based on their ethnic origin. His fervent hope was that people of every nation, race, and language would unite in worshipping the God of Israel as the God of the world, in keeping with the utterances of one of Israel's most well-known and oft-quoted prophets.[5] How sad it is, therefore, to see how divided the followers of Jesus have been throughout history, and still are today. It is not what Jesus or Paul would have wanted.

The apostle Paul can be a bit of a cipher. Those who give any thought to the matter either love him or hate him. Their love is rooted in the beauty of his doctrinal pronouncements, his masterful use of the Greek language to describe faith, and his willingness to admit his faults and failings. Much of the hate directed toward Paul arises from grossly unfair attempts to hold him to modern cultural standards and behavior. He had the audacity, his opponents fulminate, to demand that Christian women in Corinth keep silent in

2. For a hilarious send-up on this, watch *Monty Python and the Holy Grail*.

3. "Then he appeared to James, then to all the apostles, and last of all he appeared to me also, as to one abnormally born" (1 Cor 15:7–8, NIV).

4. "For you have heard of my previous way of life in Judaism, how intensely I persecuted the church of God and tried to destroy it" (Gal 1:13, NIV).

5. "And foreigners who bind themselves to the LORD to minister to him, to love the name of the LORD, and to be his servants, all who keep the Sabbath without desecrating it and who hold fast to my covenant—these I will bring to my holy mountain and give them joy in my house of prayer. Their burnt offerings and sacrifices will be accepted on my altar; for my house will be called a house of prayer for all nations" (Isa 56:6–7, NIV).

church and hold no authority over men. Tsk, tsk. Never mind that Paul seems to have regarded a considerable number of women as his equals in ministry, and that his pronouncements about women dealt with specific situations in a specific community. Some of the criticism leveled against Paul may flow out of the perception that he is at least partially at fault for the mess that Christianity is in. I admit that I spent time in that camp, but recent study convinced me to take a different view. Regardless of what he may have intended, those who subsequently twisted Paul's words to suit needs that were far removed from what he intended have caused much of the damage done in his name.

It is not my intent to defend Paul or his words; I will leave that to the experts. My point is that Paul's missionary efforts in the Greek-speaking, non-Jewish world had the unintended consequence of laying a foundation for institutional Christianity, a construct far different from what I believe Jesus intended. Paul unwittingly helped draw up the blueprints for a Trojan horse that, in time, morphed into institutional Christianity. Some who received and accepted Paul's teaching misunderstood it or deliberately distorted it for their own ends. This led in short order (less than three centuries) to the usurpation of a simple faith-movement by an onerous, complex, and increasingly autocratic institution focused on doctrinal conformity and political survival. I know that sounds heretical, but questions need to be posed in view of what institutional Christianities have done in the name of Christ in the past and what they have become and are doing in these "enlightened" times. The alternative is to believe that internecine warfare between Christians over doctrinal differences, brutal wars in Italy, the Crusades, the Spanish Inquisition, horrific persecutions of Christians by other Christians, and various other atrocities were all part of Jesus' plan. I refuse to blame Jesus for the failings of his alleged followers.

Paul's own words reveal his belief that his God-given mission was to proclaim to the non-Jewish (Gentile) populace that a Jewish Messiah loved them enough to die for them and thereby save them from eternal death. This alone, given Paul's Jewishness and his status within Judaism, is extraordinary. Yet, the nagging doubt remains: Did Paul cut corners in the name of expediency in ways that led to the creation of something other than what either he or Jesus intended? Hear what I am *not* saying. I am not saying that Jesus could not and did not make use of Paul, other Christians, and the church (even at its worst) to accomplish his purposes and carry out his mission. What I *am* saying is that the time has come for a major reevaluation of what it means to be the church and to seriously consider that it is time for the institutional Christianities of the world to give way to a simple, diverse movement of *people* instsead of continuing to exist as dysfunctional corporate behemoths focused mostly on institutional survival. Christians survived and thrived three hundred years, despite sporadic persecution, in small communities spread all over the Roman Empire. Christianity was a relatively simple faith until the government got involved. Thereafter the situation grew increasingly complicated and nasty. Christianity has not been the same since then, all reformations notwithstanding.

This is unfortunate given that Paul appears to have been all about keeping it simple. I say this despite that fact that countless books have been written and many careers built on the assertion that his theology is deeply complex and therefore inaccessible to most people. Those in leadership have always used this to control the lives and beliefs of the faithful—even after the Protestant Reformation introduced the radical notion that every believer was free to read and interpret the Bible without help from experts. The truth is that Paul is easy to understand, given a few simple keys. These keys are easily found in the Scriptures and the Jewish teachings and beliefs of the first century AD. Even those passages that seem to depend heavily on Greek philosophy are best understood in a Hebrew context. Paul may have been the apostle to the Gentiles, but he never stopped being a Jew in his beliefs about God and his faith in Jesus as the Savior of the world. This is most easily observed in his letter to the church in Rome.

> I am talking to you Gentiles. Inasmuch as I am the apostle to the Gentiles, I take pride in my ministry in the hope that I may somehow arouse my own people to envy and save some of them.
>
> —PAUL OF JESUS[6]

It is to our benefit that Paul did not establish the Christian community in Rome. The letter he wrote to the Roman church is the closest we have to a systematic exposition of his theology. One element stands out. In presenting his bona fides to the Christians in Rome prior to his visit Paul called himself "an apostle to the Gentiles." The record of Paul's missionary journeys preserved in his writings and the Acts of the Apostles show that his evangelistic focus was the Greek-speaking world, a world with which he was intimately familiar. In all fairness, Paul was uniquely suited to this role given his birth in Tarsus and education in Jerusalem. You might say that he was the obvious choice for the job. You see, he could claim to be both a citizen of the Roman world and a faithful, observant Jew. It was a double-edged sword. Gentiles accused him of favoring Jews and Jews accused him of favoring Gentiles, and everyone ridiculed him because he was short, balding, and unattractive. The latter is one reason why Paul is my hero. People still place far too much emphasis on physical appearance as an indication of worth. Institutions

6. Rom 11:13–14, NIV.

tend to prefer and promote the most photogenic leaders, irrespective of any other qualifications, despite the clear admonition of Scripture to disregard outward appearances. Paul's weakness in that area hindered him in some places and helped him in others.

There are no accidental words in the Bible. If the Bible reports that Paul was a native of Tarsus, it must be important. The history of Tarsus, located in present-day Turkey, goes back at least six millennia. We know that it passed through Hittite, Assyrian, Persian, and Greek control before falling to the Romans at the hands of Pompey in 67 BC. It retained its Greek character during Roman rule. Romans hated Greeks but loved their culture, and regularly employed Greek slaves as tutors, teachers, physicians, and scribes. Paul, whose birth name was Saul, was a Roman citizen, a Jew by birth, and Greek by education and culture. He had a good grasp of Roman law, thought, history, and customs. Educated in all things Jewish by a rabbi named Gamaliel (according to tradition) in Jerusalem, Saul impressed his teachers enough to rise quickly in the ranks of the party of the Pharisees. His familiarity with Greek philosophy stood him in good stead, but he did not boast about his Roman citizenship among his Jewish compatriots, preferring to keep it in his back pocket, as it were, until it could help him get out of a tight spot.[7]

Saul of Tarsus, before he became Paul of Jesus, was a high-ranking Pharisee on the fast track to the top. In stating this we must avoid evaluating Paul using the one-dimensional portrait of the Pharisees painted by the Gospel writers. There were two opposing "schools" of Pharisaic thought in those days. We have no clear idea which one Saul/Paul identified with, but his actions prior to conversion indicate that he held closely to the "right-wing conservative" branch.[8] This branch of Pharisaism held to a literal interpretation of the Law and was opposed to Gentiles converting to Judaism unless the potential convert could prove he had a genealogical connection to a verifiable Jewish ancestor. After he "saw the light" when he met the risen Jesus on the road to Damascus, his writings indicate an affinity for the more "liberal" of the two,[9] although he also espoused views that reflected his conservative background. Interestingly, the teachings of Jesus also place him, though not completely, in the liberal camp. But I digress.

---

7. As they stretched him out to flog him, Paul said to the centurion standing there, "Is it legal for you to flog a Roman citizen who hasn't even been found guilty?" When the centurion heard this, he went to the commander and reported it. "What are you going to do?" he asked. "This man is a Roman citizen." The commander went to Paul and asked, "Tell me, are you a Roman citizen?" "Yes, I am," he answered (Acts 22:25–27, NIV).

8. The school of Shammai (50 BC–AD 30).

9. The school of Hillel (110 BC–AD 10).

The point is that Paul could not help being influenced by his early upbringing in a predominantly Greek environment. Finding certain doors closed following his conversion, it is only natural that he turned to the people most likely to welcome him with less suspicion. If one door closed it meant that God wanted him to go through a different one.[10] Paul could expect a less than favorable reception in Jerusalem, which may have helped him in his efforts to reach out to the Jews outside of Palestine. There was, to put it mildly, some hard feelings between the urbane, cultured Jews in the big city and the rustic, unsophisticated ones out in the country. In any case, the accounts of Paul's conversion, one in the third person and one in the first,[11] both explicitly state that he believed his Jesus-ordained mission was to the Gentile world. Paul carried out his mission with dedication and zeal, preaching and teaching throughout Asia Minor and possibly even in Europe. He planted Christian communities all over the region. Paul's writings make it clear that he firmly believed that Jesus offered salvation to the entire world on behalf of the God of Israel. Some of his colleagues in the ranks of the Pharisees judged this as a heresy deserving of death. Some Gentiles to whom he preached saw little reason to repudiate their ancestral gods even if they were willing to consider what Paul had to say. Emperor Constantine (AD 306–337), who can legitimately be called the "Patron Saint of the Institutional Church," saw no contradiction in maintaining his faith in the Sun-god of his ancestral faith while also supporting and promoting empire-wide dedication to the Son of God worshipped by his Christian subjects. Religious decisions in the ancient world were different than they are today, at least in the Western world. Everyone at least publicly acknowledged the existence of divine beings, regardless of their private beliefs. Anyone who claimed to be an atheist was deemed a fool at best or, as was more usually considered the case, dangerously insane.[12]

> For I resolved to know nothing while I was with you except Jesus
> Christ and him crucified.
>
> —Paul of Jesus[13]

Paul intentionally and sincerely reframed a Jewish message in ways that the sophisticated and cultured Greeks would listen to and hopefully accept. He resolved to keep the message simple, but some of his followers refused

---

10. And when they had come up to Mysia, they attempted to go into Bithynia, but the Spirit of Jesus did not allow them (Acts 16:7, ESV).

11. Acts 9:1–16; Gal 1:11–16.

12. The fool says in his heart, "There is no God" (Psalm 53:1, ESV).

13. 1 Cor 2:2, NIV.

to accept that anything worth believing could be as basic as the gospel Paul proclaimed. They insisted on adding "special knowledge" to the gospel proclamation that was only accessible to a select group. Despite the diligent efforts of Paul and others over the course of a generation or so, this continued to be a problem, one that echoed down through the centuries even after the Corinthian church (where the problem was most pronounced) ceased to exist. Some who inherited Paul's teaching and the philosophical barnacles that clung to it used it to formulate doctrines and make statements that have resulted in the persecution, torture, and death of countless people over the centuries, many of whom sincerely believed that they held to the ancient faith as handed down directly from the apostles. For example, Paul's words were also used to justify the formation and financial support of an institutional clergy class. The clergy class accrued to itself a level of worldly status and power to which Jesus himself never aspired. Violent contention erupted in the Middle Ages over the question of whether Jesus owned the clothes he wore. The church argued in the affirmative, thereby justifying its ownership of much more than a simple robe. Much damage has been done and continues to be done by those who believe their status as clergy affords them a high degree of prestige, privilege, power, and wealth. They demand that those they claim to serve reward them lavishly, then point to their prosperity as a sign of God's approval and blessing. Meanwhile children mere blocks away from their luxurious mansions die of starvation daily. I read recently of a Roman Catholic bishop who chose not to move into the $2.4 million mansion his diocese built for him to live in after his retirement because it would look bad (duh!). I wonder what they will do with that mansion.

Make no mistake, there is much in the writings of Paul that is edifying. In some ways it is unfortunate that Paul wrote his letters in Greek, sometimes using philosophical terms. Yet, he is not the problem. Rather, it is his followers who used his sincere effort to explain Eastern thought using Western ideas in ways that caused needless argument and controversy, helping to generate incomprehensible theological pronouncements that the faithful are exhorted to accept as "mysteries." They are philosophical nonsense. Let me give you an example.

> We believe in one Lord, Jesus Christ, the only Son of God, eternally begotten of the Father, God from God, Light from Light, true God from true God, begotten, not made, consubstantial with the Father.
>
> —FROM THE NICENE CREED, PARA. 2

Many Christians unquestioningly believe (even if they do not completely understand) the declaration that Jesus is "consubstantial (one in being) with the Father (God)." It is an essential part of the doctrine of the Trinity, asserting that Jesus is truly God and truly one with God at the same time. First declared authoritative by the Council of Nicaea in AD 325, it did not appear out of thin air; rather it intentionally replaced an older, widely held belief, identified as Arianism, that Jesus was not "eternally begotten of the Father." Arians believed that the new formulation placed too little emphasis on Jesus' humanity. Therefore, they asserted that the Father created (begot) him prior to the Creation as the means of creation. Justification for this belief was rooted in a verse from Proverbs: "The LORD created me at the beginning of His course as the first of His works of old."[14] Nicaea declared this heretical, but the belief hung on among large numbers of Christians and is still around today among a tiny minority. The proponents of the Nicaean position were in the minority, but they had the ear of the Emperor Constantine despite his personal preference for the Arian view. He promoted the non-Arian position because the bishops who were its most vocal supporters exercised control over the most powerful cities in the empire. While the anti-Arians won the day, when Constantine finally accepted baptism on his deathbed, it was an Arian bishop, Eusebius of Nicomedia, who did the honors. Subsequent emperors likewise supported the Nicaean faction despite their personal belief in Arianism.

Why is this important? As I have already stated; nowhere in the words of Jesus do I find a statement about the necessity of believing in doctrine for salvation. Yet that is what institutional Christianities and their representatives incessantly demand as the condition for avoiding eternal damnation. In the past this demand was enforced by torture and death. It was a no-win situation for the accused since both confessing and the refusal to confess resulted in death. The only (subtle) difference was that the former left open the possibility of eternal salvation while the latter ensured damnation. The most basic problem here is that doctrines are fallible assertions created by fallible human beings, often for fallible reasons. They have no power to save; in fact, they have no power at all. They are, at best, a species of "Trojan Horse" in that they promise a reward (salvation) they are incapable of bestowing. We must get back to the basics. This means setting aside our prejudices, pretensions, and presuppositions. We need to let Jesus be Jesus, not insist that Jesus fit into the world view or the set of doctrines we favor. Doctrine is like money: it is morally neutral but can be used for both good and evil. When it is wielded by those who desire power over others it becomes a weapon of mass dissension

14. Prov 8:22, TNK.

and destruction. Doctrine attempts to define the truth and fit Jesus into a specific theological framework. This is idolatry. Instead, we need to let Jesus speak the truth, regardless of how uncomfortable it might be to hear.

The apostle Paul helps us in this if we are willing to set aside preconceptions about his message and motives. The early church preserved enough of Paul's letters to give us a good picture of the struggles he faced in his efforts to convince people of the truth of what he preached and taught. To Paul's credit, he began almost all his missionary efforts by visiting the local synagogue. This often overlooked element of his work serves as a reminder that Paul retained his connection to Judaism as he sought to reframe the significance of Jesus' death and resurrection in terms and concepts the Greek world could comprehend and accept as true. He helpfully boiled the gospel down to its most basic elements:

> For I delivered to you as of first importance what I also received: that *Christ died for our sins* in accordance with the Scriptures, that *he was buried*, that *he was raised on the third day* in accordance with the Scriptures, and that *he appeared* to Cephas, then to the twelve. Then he appeared to more than five hundred brothers at one time, most of whom are still alive, though some have fallen asleep. Then he appeared to James, then to all the apostles. Last of all, as to one untimely born, he appeared also to me.
>
> —PAUL OF JESUS[15]

The italicized words are the essence of Paul's teaching. The phrase "in accordance with the Scriptures" appears after the most important assertions. Christians must remember that this phrase refers exclusively to the Hebrew Bible, not the writings that came to be the Christians Scriptures (the New Testament). These statements *must* be understood within the context of Judaism, specifically the sacrificial system, if we are to uncover their true meaning.

Paul began his missionary efforts zealously, seeking out the people in every community he believed would help him further his plans. He visited the synagogues, often focusing some of his attention on the wealthiest and most influential citizens. In one sense Paul had no choice, and, to be fair, there is some evidence to suggest that Jesus relied on the patronage of "wealthy" families to support him. Jesus was not, so far as we know, accused of any impropriety in this area. In fact, the opposite appears to be the case. The ruling classes of Judaism took umbrage at Jesus' willingness to mingle with the lower classes and those they deemed unworthy of either attention

---

15. 1 Cor 15:3–8, ESV.

or salvation. He and his followers kept a common purse from which their expenses were paid, and alms were given to the poor. It is interesting that the purse was managed by Judas Iscariot, the disciple who betrayed Jesus into the hands of the authorities. He did so on the promise of a reward of thirty pieces of silver. Make of that what you will.

Jesus' integrity in the matter of finances is apparent in that he was able to take people to task over their attitudes and use of money without being charged with hypocrisy. Paul, however, was not immune to attacks on his associations with the wealthy. On one occasion, he indignantly informed the church in Corinth that he had relied only on his own work as a maker and repairer of tents to support himself,[16] but their accusations that he accepted money from wealthy patrons must have some basis in fact. Paul's defense of his actions in Corinth includes his assertion that those who work full-time preaching and teaching the gospel deserve compensation that is fair and reasonable. This has been used throughout the history of institutional Christianity to support and defend the existence of a professional clergy class. I have been a member of that class for nearly three decades. Experience has taught me that pastors who rely upon those to whom they are preaching the gospel for financial support face a potential conflict of interest. Regardless of the real motivations behind the giving and receiving of financial gifts, even as a means of support, the natural perception is that favors are granted or expected along with the exchange. The same is true today. Relatively few pastors are compensated at a level commensurate with those in the secular realm who have a similar level of education and experience. This will continue to be a problem so long as divine blessing is equated with wealth and members of the clergy are equated with the professional class.

Paul, wittingly or unwittingly, set a pattern still being followed today. Some church leaders routinely seek out affluent members to help build their ecclesiastical empires, and the affluent members in turn expect a degree of influence in the direction and work of the institution. If this is done anonymously and with purity of heart and purpose, it can result in amazing things being accomplished for the cause of Jesus. I have seen godly people with a godly perspective on money generously meet a need without any desire for recognition. This is not always the case. Money is used to influence mission and direction, or to provide extra perks for pastors. The lure of wealth, and the power and prestige that come with it, has led some religious leaders to abandon their principles and follow the money. After all, why would Jesus deny them mansions, luxury cars, a sailboat, a country club membership, and the finest that life has to offer? Jesus had all this and

16. First Cor 9:15. See also Acts 18:1–3.

more. Wait, no, he did not. All he owned when he died was the robe he wore. He was stripped of that and hung *naked* on a cross.

Influential and educated Christians built upon Paul's evangelistic efforts and transformed a Jewish reformation movement into a Greek religion rife with superstition, polluted by political infighting, and beholden to pagans for support and protection. It had dire consequences for the church that continue to the present day. The blame for this must not be laid entirely at the feet of the church. Beginning with the reign of the Emperor Constantine, styled "the Great" and declared a saint by the Catholic Church, church and government were inextricably intertwined, each using the other to gain, power, influence, and supremacy. Emperors who had little or no concern for religious matters, and little education in theological matters, routinely settled religious disputes based on who made the best case or could provide the most influence in return, as we have observed. There were seven church councils between AD 325 and AD 787, all of them convoked by emperors more concerned with political unity than doctrinal or theological integrity. Their aim in every instance was to enforce conformity to a specific doctrine while claiming to be working only to establish the truth. The problem is that these doctrines contribute little if anything to the work of the gospel as Jesus described it. Once Nicaean Christianity became the official religion of the Roman Empire, establishing correct doctrine and enforcing adherence to it became far more important than the work of the gospel: demonstrating mercy and compassion and proclaiming the promise of eternal life in and through Jesus. This is just as true today. Imagine how much good could be done in the world if institutional Christianity dismantled its top-heavy bureaucracies, sold its administrative campuses, disbanded all its churches, and devoted all its time and energy to doing good in the world?

> If Christ were here there is one thing he would not be—a Christian.
>
> —MARK TWAIN[17]

My experience has shown me that many Christians are woefully ignorant of doctrine and naïvely assume that "all Christians pretty much believe the same things." I cannot begin to count the number of times I heard people say this to me with absolute sincerity, expecting me to affirm it. This is not only uninformed; it is insulting to those who struggled mightily, often risking their health, their possessions, and their lives, to counter the prevailing beliefs of their time and reform the church. Fundamental differences divide Roman from Orthodox Catholics, Catholics from Protestants, and different

17. https://www.azquotes.com/quote/367867.

Protestant faiths from one another. Martin Luther (Lutheranism) spent time in exile before returning to his native land. John Calvin (Presbyterianism) was born in France but lived, worked, and died in exile in Switzerland. The Puritans were exiled from England to America after they attempted to "purify" the Church of England of its "Catholic" practices. My ancestors fled from Switzerland to Alsace-Loraine in the seventeenth century to escape Catholic persecution, which I find amusing since I grew up Roman Catholic. These are just a few examples of how seriously some of our forebears took doctrinal differences.

The institutional Christianities of the world have no more hope of being united in any meaningful way than do the political factions in America, all ecumenical efforts notwithstanding. Those on the extremes rule the debate. One end of the spectrum insists that they alone are faithful to the expression of the faith handed down by the apostles and that everyone else is apostate, heretical, and bound for hell. There are those on the opposite end of the spectrum who claim that every denomination, indeed every religion, is true in its own way and offers an equally valid path to heaven, if that is where you want to go when you die. In the middle are the people who simply do not care one way or the other, and who find all this wrangling about doctrine and theology tiresome, meaningless, and a waste of time. The churches that are thriving are either those who offer the best programs with the least level of commitment and little challenge to change one's behavior, or those who demand an elevated level of commitment and adherence to a rigid set of rules. Denominations find themselves "reorganizing for better stewardship of their resources" which is a convenient euphemism for getting by with less. One middle governing body in a dying denomination of which I was a part was always in the process of reorganization. Every two years they would feel the need to come up with a new organizational structure which, after it was instituted, would then form a committee to come up with a new structure to be implemented in two years. This is what I call rearranging the deck chairs on the Titanic.

Institutional Christianities in the modern world are Greeks bearing gifts that few people seem to desire. The Trojan Horse they offer is the assertion that you can be a Christian and get to heaven without making any significant changes to your life. In fact, you can pick and choose the words of Jesus you want to accept and reject the ones that do not work for you. If you find that you are unhappy, it is undoubtedly because someone is rejecting you or the lifestyle you chose to live. Jesus wants most for you to be happy and loved, and you are free to define love in whatever way you choose. There are a multitude of problems with this, but the most obvious is with how the institutional church defines love. If we are to take Jesus at his word, then love is first and foremost sacrificial; it is about what I give, not what I get. More than this, true love has little or nothing to do with sexual intercourse. Any suggestion to the contrary debases the whole idea of love, especially as it pertains to God's love for us. The "gift" that progressive Christianity in the West wants to give us is the lie that any action can be justified in the name of love and can therefore do no harm. I find it more than a little fascinating that the more educated proponents of this view point to the ancient Greeks as their role model. Where is that civilization now?

It may be, as I have stated in this chapter, that the apostle Paul's efforts to share the gospel with the Greek-speaking world had the unintended consequence of planting the seeds from which institutional Christianity grew. Yet, there is more to the story. The failure to think ahead and attempt to discern the future consequences of one's actions has led to many disasters. The same is true of institutional Christianity. It is limping down the road to hell, but why? Let us look at some of the decisions that, perhaps, led to this unintended consequence.

Chapter 6

The Road to Hell is Paved with Unintended Consequences

> We must always be careful of the actions we take, for there are always unintended consequences. Sometimes they are serendipitous, other times they are appalling, but those consequences are always there. We must tread lightly in this world. . .until we are sure of foot.
>
> —NEAL SHUSTERMAN, *UNDIVIDED*[1]

It is said that no good deed goes unpunished. This is related to the law of unintended consequences: Human actions have effects that are unanticipated or unplanned. History is filled with examples. Unintended consequences occur because the results of an action are easier to see in hindsight than to anticipate or predict ahead of time. When you combine this law with the well-known aphorism, "The road to hell is paved with good intentions," you arrive at the title of this chapter. Human nature being what it is, it is inevitable that actions taken with the best of intentions and the purest motives will have unintended consequences, not all of them positive or beneficial. A common response in the aftermath of a disastrous unintended consequence is to pledge to learn something from the mistake, apply it to the present, and strive to do better in the future. This is a nice thought, but not realistic given humanity's propensity to ignore the lessons of the past and blindly plunge headlong into the future. After all, we proud denizens of the present are far more advanced in every area than the benighted and ill-informed inhabitants of the past, right? Wrong.

---

1. https://www.goodreads.com/quotes/6776380-we-must-always-be-careful-of-the-actions-we-take.

The temptation to view the past one-dimensionally is ever-present, especially the further one delves into it. Here is an example. Casual historians and scholars like to describe the early church as a cohesive, united, and uniform body. This was true only in the narrowest sense. The geographically scattered communities of Jesus followers in the first three centuries after his death were not completely unified in practice or doctrine, nor did they view such unity as essential. The earliest communities shared a common understanding of the crucial elements of the gospel proclamation, but other assertions were up for grabs. This vagueness arose in part from the fact that the first generation of believers were mostly Jews, which meant that they naturally viewed Jesus and his message through the lens of Jewish belief. This changed as the first generation died off and the number of non-Jewish converts accelerated. Christian leaders eventually arrived at the (mistaken) belief that the survival of the movement was inseparably linked to uniformity of doctrine and practice across the world. While this was laudable, it was both unrealistic and unnecessary because it sought to enforce beliefs that had little or nothing to do with the core message of the gospel. Their efforts were less than successful in part because their methods for attaining uniformity were usually inconsistent with Christian belief and practice, especially after the first generation of believers died. As their power and influence in the world grew, the largest groups of Christians in the most influential urban centers sought to enforce doctrinal unity among all Christians by any means, even if it meant that some followers of Jesus were persecuted, imprisoned, and even killed for refusing to go along with the dominant position. The result was further division that became entrenched because of the methods utilized by the victors. This did not change with the passage of time.

> It is . . . highly probable that from the very beginning, apart from
> death, the only ironclad rule of human experience has been the
> Law of Unintended Consequences.
>
> —Ian Tattersall[2]

The quest for completely unified belief and purpose is fraught with danger, which does not stop humanity from trying to achieve it. This is especially true when the effort is undertaken by organizations and institutions, large and small. Institutions demand uniformity because it is vital to their structural health and success. But is it a necessary part of *religious* belief and practice? Is uniformity of doctrine necessary in an unstructured movement? The early church was, after all, a simple, humble movement

---

2. https://www.azquotes.com/quote/745205.

when it began in the towns and villages of Judea and Galilee. The message was simple: God wants you to be part of his forever family, and sent Jesus to extend the invitation and bring you in. Believe that Jesus is your Savior, repent of your sins, and you are assured of eternal life. Then be baptized in his name and live according to his commandments. The promise of eternal life was vitally important in a world where death was often violent, sudden, ever-present, and widely believed to be the end of existence. God opened the door to eternal life when he raised Jesus from the dead. This is the basic message of the gospel. There was no need to demand uniformity of doctrine at the earliest stages of Christian witness because there were only two possible answers to the question of whether one believed in Jesus for salvation: yes, or no. It may be that the simplicity of this endeavor had the unintended consequence of allowing the development and proliferation of an abundance of different understandings about Jesus, which in turn led to the births of multiple groups all claiming to have the definitive one.

The issues here are countless. Even as the first Christian missionaries gained converts from Jewish communities outside of Palestine, so too missionaries working in the cities and towns of Asia Minor gained non-Jewish converts. Their good intention was to extend a Jewish Messiah's invitation of salvation to a Gentile[3] world. An unintended consequence was that non-Jewish converts filtered the gospel message through their philosophical beliefs, resulting in a hybrid faith that soon strayed from what Jesus taught and intended. The earliest expressed beliefs about Jesus in his messianic identity indicate that the (Jewish) church regarded him as a human being set apart by God and revealed as the Messiah/Savior by his resurrection.[4] Jewish belief simply would not allow Jesus to be God or to be equal with him in any way. The notion of a "triune godhead" only became possible (and perhaps even necessary) when Jewish theology and Greek philosophy were merged into what I can only describe as an unholy alliance. The unintended consequence of this, in turn, was that a simple religion focused on salvation through a relationship with a person soon became a complex religious-philosophical system that demanded acceptance of a set of specific systematic doctrines as a starting point on a long, arduous path to the unguaranteed possibility of salvation.

I have been arguing that institutional Christianities in the Western world are in a bad way these days. There is still enough optimism in my soul to make me want to believe that those who launched Christianity down

---

3. From the perspective of Judaism, a Gentile was anyone who was not ethnically Jewish.

4. Norris, *Christological Controversy*, 2.

this path did so with good—indeed the best of—intentions. It is somewhat helpful to analyze what happened, and perhaps even to fix some blame, but once this is complete the best course of action is to figure out what needs to happen next. If we are to avoid the mistakes and missteps of the past, we need to learn how the religious institutions that identify as Christian came to be in the state they are in today. I believe that while Christian thinkers and leaders throughout history acted with good intentions, their approach was not always spiritually beneficial, and led to more harm than good in a fair number of cases. It all depends on how you define the word "good."

> A good intention, with a bad approach, often leads to a poor result.
>
> —Thomas A. Edison[5]

The road to hell may be paved with good intentions, but the ramifications are mediated to some degree by the fact that the word "good" is relative. It is fair to say that attempts to establish and impose uniformity of belief and doctrine throughout history have been characterized as good by those who have led them. The Arian controversy mentioned earlier is just one example. The first fifteen centuries of the church's existence are depressingly filled with examples of Christians persecuting Christians, especially after Constantine gave the victors the power to vanquish their doctrinal enemies using the prosecutorial, executorial, and military powers of the state. We must be fair, however, and note that Protestants have just as vigorously hounded, persecuted, and exterminated their own kind in the name of the good intention of establishing and maintaining doctrinal purity. The Anabaptist movement, which began in Zurich around the same time Martin Luther was starting a theological debate in Germany, was persecuted initially by the Roman Catholic Church, but also faced violent opposition from Protestants, including Lutherans and Calvinists, based primarily on its assertion that infant baptism was not supported by Scripture. The focus of the argument was whether baptism is required for salvation to be effective. (It is not.)

It can be safely (although arguably) stated that the Protestant Reformation did not begin with the best of intentions. The opening volley was fired when Henry VIII of England decided to break from Rome and assumed authority over the churches in his country so that he could grant himself an ecclesiastical divorce. His success opened a Pandora's box of ills. Henry's assertion that he was acting in the best interests of the faith and the faithful (untrue) was seized upon by powers across Europe to separate themselves

---

5. https://www.azquotes.com/quote/1351361.

from a corrupt, money-hungry institutional bureaucracy in Rome. Some
of the supporting cast, many of them nominally Christian at best, cynically
seized on the movement as a chance to increase their power, wealth, and
influence over the much hated and maligned papacy. In rejecting the Pope's
claim to supreme spiritual and biblical authority, the Reformers created a
power vacuum that begged to be filled. In my opinion, there are no truly
leaderless societies or organizations, or at least none that lasted long. This
is just as true of religious organizations as it is of those in the secular realm.
In a time when secular and spiritual authority were often intertwined and
largely indistinguishable, it was imperative that the fragments breaking off
from the institutional Christianities of the day have recognized leaders, otherwise no one would take them seriously. This was as true in the beginning
as it was then and is today. Allow me a short digression.

> How very profitable this fable of Christ has been to us through
> the ages.
>
> —GIOVANNI DE' MEDICI, POPE LEO X[6]

The story of the Jesus movement in the Bible does not end with the
Gospel accounts of Jesus' life and ministry. Luke wrote a sequel to his Gospel
called the "Acts of the Apostles." It contains some remarkable stories, a few
of them quite humorous,[7] but it is unclear as to the process the first community of Jesus followers used to fill the leadership position he left vacant. The
only evidence that Jesus may have had a succession plan is found in Matthew 16:18–19.[8] This oft-misinterpreted statement has led to the mistaken
assumption that Jesus intended for Peter to "rule the church" as its leader
when the time came. An obvious problem with this is that the church at its
earliest stage was a loosely organized community whose members were held
together by their shared loyalty to Jesus, not by an established institutional
structure. The Greek word translated "church" in the passage cited above
first meant a community, a gathering, or an assembly. It was only later that
the term was used to designate what became the institutional church. The
focus, in any case, is on Peter's declaration of faith that Jesus was "the Christ
[Messiah], the Son of the living God"[9] that is the "rock" upon which the
church is to be built and by which it is to be sustained. Having accepted

6. Quoted in Chamberlin, *Bad Popes*, 223.

7. Acts 20:7–10—falling asleep during a sermon can be deadly!

8. Jesus: "And I tell you, you are Peter, and on this rock I will build my church, and
the gates of hell shall not prevail against it. I will give you the keys of the kingdom of
heaven, and whatever you bind on earth shall be bound in heaven, and whatever you
loose on earth shall be loosed in heaven."

9. Matt 16:16.

the new normal of a Jesus-directed mission that did not include Jesus as its physically present leader, the first community of Jesus followers needed to decide who would take over the role that Jesus had held.

This is where things get a little complicated for some. While the evidence shows that Peter played a pivotal role in the early development of the faith community, its leader was clearly James, Jesus' brother. Family ties carried a lot of weight in the ancient world. Jesus' inner circle was not immune to this phenomenon. Peter and Andrew were brothers, as were James and John, the sons of Zebedee. Although Jesus' family initially refused to believe in him,[10] by the end of his ministry some of them were on board. Jesus' inner circle was mainly Galilean, as was his family.[11] Cultural expectations dictated that a family member would take over for Jesus in the exercise of authority over the community he founded and continue his mission. This goes against Catholic tradition, doctrine, and belief, but there is no mistaking the evidence clearly presented in the Bible that, at best, Peter was one of three men who held the reins of power in the early church in a kind of triumvirate. He, along with James and John, were Jesus' inner-inner circle, the ones to whom Jesus seems to have entrusted special teaching and attention (a point emphasized in the Gospel of John).

The nascent Jesus movement, if it was to survive into the future as a viable, growing faith community, needed a leader. James the brother of Jesus was the natural choice given the family relationship and his status as one of Jesus' inner-circle. James led this community from Jerusalem, not Rome because Jerusalem is where Jesus died, and it was the spiritual focal point of Judaism, which was the faith of Jesus and his followers. It is clear from the chronology of the letters of Paul that the church in Rome was a late addition; the churches in Asia Minor were founded earlier. The Roman Catholic Church asserts that the supreme governance of the "Church" began in Rome. In one sense this is true, but only after the passage of several centuries and intervention by an arguably pagan Roman emperor. Even then, recognition of Rome as the central authority of the church happened only after decades of wrangling and division.

Let us not forget that Jesus was a Jew born into a Jewish family. He grew up in Galilee, recruited fellow Jews (mostly Galileans) to be his followers, preached to Jews and taught in Jewish synagogues (mostly in Galilee). Why, then, would anyone believe that the early church would immediately shift the seat of its authority from Judea to Rome? There is, to be sure, a connection between Peter and Rome. According to both legend and tradition,

---

10. "For not even his brothers believed in him" (John 7:5).

11. Nazareth was, and is, in Galilee.

Peter was crucified in Rome in AD 64 in the reign of Nero (whose insanely cruel persecutions included Christians being burned alive as torches to illuminate banquets at evening festivals),[12] but there is no evidence that Peter held a leadership role in the city, let alone universal authority over a church and hierarchy that did not yet exist. The bishop of Rome eventually claimed supreme authority over the church, but not because of Jesus; it rested on the convenient fiction that Peter had ruled the church from there and passed that authority down to those who were duly elected in his place. This would be laughable if not for the atrocities perpetrated over the centuries to support and further this claim, as well as the claim that the bishop of Rome held the authority to appoint and depose emperors, kings, and princes, as well as to divide up newly discovered continents.[13]

The communities that coalesced into the Roman Catholic Church retained a degree of autonomy from the bishop of Rome until shortly after the reign of Constantine, who with visions of empire dancing in his head and in a bid to curry divine favor on his way to conquering much of the known world, promised (according to legend) to convert to Christianity if the Christian God would aid him in the battle. As luck would have it, Constantine won the day, more through military skill and tactical supremacy on the battlefield than divine assistance, I suspect. I struggle with the notion that God intentionally sought the ruin that Constantine subsequently visited upon the church by legitimizing it as the official religion of his empire, even if he did not follow it religiously, if you will allow me the pun. Constantine added insult to injury when he claimed the authority to moderate and pass judgment on theological and doctrinal disputes with only the most cursory understanding of the concepts involved. Constantine relied on the opinions of others, supporting those who flattered him the most, promised the most, made the most compelling promises regarding his legacy, or guaranteed religious peace and unity throughout the empire. Constantine "gave" the church freedom from persecution, but it did more harm than good.

Even if we assume that Constantine's "gift" of recognition to the church was made with every good intention, it eventually contributed to an environment in which the powers of Europe blindly accepted as genuine a pernicious forged document that "suddenly" appeared centuries after Constantine was dead describing a gift he never would have given. His good intention, along with that forged document, paved the road that led into a hellish period in history when the church, Italy, and the rest of Europe

---

12. Champlin, *Nero*, 121.

13. Pope Alexander VI, who reigned from 1492 to 1503, arbitrarily divided possession of the "New World" between Spain and France.

plunged into a period of darkness lasting well into modern times. Constantine, an adherent to Arianism, cared less for determining theological orthodoxy than he did for maintaining peace in his empire. Having abandoned malarial, marshy, dilapidated Rome, he built the magnificent eastern city of Constantinople and established it as the new seat of the Roman Empire. Even though he situated his capitol in the East, Constantine expected the provincials in the backwaters of the West to pay their taxes in full and on time and not rebel against his authority. This worked until certain church leaders, coveting the power not only to defeat but to destroy their opponents, dragged Constantine into their theological battles. Personal wealth and political power were more important to them than eliminating the stench of hypocrisy that enveloped Christianity and Christians because of their actions. This, in my opinion, contributed to the split between Eastern and Western Christendom and helped give rise not only to the Church of England and the Protestant Reformation, but also to Islam.

The forged document to which I am referring is the *Donation of Constantine*, written by a papal official named Christophorous in the early-to-mid eighth century. It claims to be the record of a decree Constantine issued in AD 315 giving the bishop of Rome authority over the ancient church centers of Alexandria, Antioch, Jerusalem, and Constantinople. In gratitude for a miracle of healing from leprosy at the hands of "Pope" Sylvester (acknowledged only as the bishop of Rome at the time), it also claims that Constantine granted the "papacy" a large swath of territory in Italy to possess and from which to derive income. Despite obvious inaccuracies in the document, it was quickly accepted as genuine and subsequently used to justify every kind of atrocity to preserve the church's possession of this "donation." Almost overnight, the papacy became a prize to be sought for the potential wealth it brought rather than as the position of the highest spiritual leader of Christianity. There is no little irony in the fact that Christophorous lost his life during a riot that erupted in AD 767 over who would succeed to the papacy after the reigning pope died, the leading families of Rome shrewdly recognizing the lucrative financial benefits of the position and violently vying with one another for the right to possess it.[14]

The road to hell is paved with unintended consequences; this is the final lesson that Christophorous learned. Intentional or not, the papacy ceased being a solely spiritual office. The men who sat on the Chair of Peter were viewed by the world as the spiritual leader of Christendom, at least in the West, but increasingly viewed themselves mainly as the temporal ruler of a swath of territories in Italy. Given human nature, it is no surprise that

14. Chamberlain, *Bad Popes*, 18.

the intoxicating lure of worldly power won out over the far less tangible rewards associated with faithfulness in the spiritual realm. Most of the men who sought the power and wealth associated with being the pontiff of the Roman Church in those days seemed to care little for the spiritual responsibilities associated with it; a few were unwilling to pay even lip service to the spiritual responsibilities of the office. Many people, especially those nearest Rome or in the highest levels of the hierarchy, knew of the corruption festering in the wretched specimens of humanity who sought the highest spiritual office in the world for the earthly rewards it would bring and clung to the papacy like hungry maggots on a corpse, but they still demanded that someone be elected to serve as the supreme leader of the Roman Church, preferably an Italian. Regardless of their personal feelings about the man who occupied the papal throne, no one was averse to seeking his favor and hoping to benefit from his largesse. It is easy to criticize their attitudes and actions, but to do so is utter hypocrisy. It is still the practice of Christians, especially those in leadership, to curry favor where they can find it and to seek power over others. There are exceptions to this, of course, but one need only note how many leaders of so-called megachurches with huge congregations and television ministries have fallen victim to pride, failed morally, turned into tyrants, or sold their soul to the devil by watering down Jesus' message if it will help them make more money.

The road to hell is paved with unintended consequences. Churches of all kinds struggle to function without financial support. I have watched pastors compromise their principles to gain favor and raise money in the name of "furthering the gospel." They may preach on it, especially during "stewardship season," but there do not seem to be many prominent pastors who sincerely believe what Jesus said about the dangers of storing up treasures on earth, at least in view of their actions.[15] Although I have strived to avoid it, I am sure that I have failed in this area as well; it is difficult to ignore the siren call of wealth, privilege, and prosperity. Naturally, I have struggled with envy as I wondered why people in vocations with no apparent eternal significance make far more than they need while many pastors, who are attempting to help people into eternity, are expected to subsist on far less. The people who have everything always seem ready to inform those who have nothing that having it all is not all it's cracked up to be, but rarely seem uncomfortable enough to give away what they do not need. This is one reason why many pastors are tempted by wealth and aspire to attain it. I

15. "Do not lay up for yourselves treasures on earth, where moth and rust destroy and where thieves break in and steal, but lay up for yourselves treasures in heaven, where neither moth nor rust destroy and where thieves do not break in and steal" (Matt 6:19–20, ESV).

freely confess that I am not immune. Wealth can be used to bless others, as I have seen and experienced, but is also an excuse to believe that God, having "blessed" someone with abundant resources, has also "blessed" that person with spiritual authority and power.

> In today's world more harm may be done by well-intentioned people trying to do good, who are unaware of the unintended consequences of their actions, than by people actually trying to cause harm.
>
> —PETER COLEMAN[16]

Unintended consequences do not respect wealth, status, or intelligence. Even the most brilliant person who sets out to do good discovers that his or her actions do not always result in what was intended. This is relevant when applied to the large historical movements that led to the current state of institutional Christianities. A case in point is the Protestant Reformation, which was started and driven by intelligent people. Henry VIII (1491–1547) was well-educated, as were most men and woman in the royal families of England. Martin Luther of Germany (1483–1546) was an educated, well-regarded lecturer and professor, especially in biblical study and interpretation. John Calvin (1509–1564) was a French lawyer and humanist who became a well-known pastor and theologian in Switzerland after breaking from the Catholic Church around 1530. Ulrich Zwingli (1484–1513) was an educated Swiss pastor whose efforts to reform Switzerland led to his death in battle at the age of forty-seven. These men helped spark a movement designed to free people from the tyranny of a religion demanding far more than its due, placing onerous burdens on them in the quest for divine acceptance, while simultaneously declaring that their hope for life after death was tenuous at best and ultimately dependent upon the judgment of the church and its representatives. The Reformers sought to place the responsibility for living a spiritually fulfilling and salvation-focused life in the hands of the individual, unmediated by any mere human being. They succeeded, but also failed, because so many human beings, when presented with a choice between good and evil, choose the latter over the former.

This leads to another unintended consequence of the Reformation: the decision to translate the Bible into the common languages of Europe. The Old Testament is comprised of documents written in Hebrew, except for the books written and added after Jerusalem fell in 586 BC.[17] The New

16.   https://www.goodreads.com/quotes/3188918-in-today-s-world-more-harm-may-be-done-by-well-intentioned.

17.   Among these are 1 and 2 Maccabees, which played a significant role in decisions made during the Reformation as to what books of the Bible were to be considered the

Testament was written in Greek. Jesus' earliest followers read the Hebrew Scriptures in a Greek translation that dates to about the third century BC.[18] Few people, apart from academicians and those with access to higher education, read the Bible in its original languages in the sixteenth century. The most common version of the Bible in use at the time of the Reformation was the Latin Vulgate, translated by a Roman Catholic scholar named Jerome in the late fourth century. To his credit, Jerome sought out Jewish rabbis in Bethlehem (at a time when his church was intentionally distancing itself from Judaism) to teach him Hebrew so that he could make an accurate translation of the Hebrew Scriptures from their original language.

The problem was that the average person did not read or understand Latin, if they were able to read at all, and therefore were unable to read the Bible. They relied on the clergy for their understanding of what the Bible taught concerning how to live and how to have any hope of spending eternity in heaven. The church forbade, on pain of death, translation of the Bible into any language other than Latin mostly because they were afraid of what would happen when "common people" read it. The pope claimed the exclusive right to determine how every verse in the Bible was interpreted. This paved the way for the promotion of non-biblical ideas, including the doctrine that whatever the pope declared to be true was as valid as the Bible. This included pronouncements about the interpretation of key biblical passages. Most people, unable to read the Bible in Latin, let alone the original languages, had to accept what they were told as fact, since to disobey the church was to risk eternal damnation.

The Reformers believed that if people had direct access to the Scriptures through careful translations into their native languages, they would be able to correctly interpret the Bible and live accordingly. Their faith in humanity was laudable but misplaced, as they soon discovered. It was not long before they began publishing commentaries that purported to provide the "correct" (read: anti-Catholic) interpretation of the Bible. This effort resulted in confusion rather than clarity for several reasons. First and foremost, every translation is an interpretation; exact translations are rarely, if ever, possible. This is exacerbated by the fact that the Bible was written in an Eastern culture, not a Western one, requiring the translator to convey the meaning of words written in a cultural context with which many readers were unfamiliar. While it is true that the Christian Scriptures were written in Greek, a Western language, the concepts contained in it are Eastern

true, inspired words of God.

18. Referred to as the Septuagint, or LXX, because according to legend, seventy scholars translated it from Hebrew independently and their translations were identical.

and therefore foreign to many westerners. This is important because it at least partially explains the proliferation of churches and denominations that plague the world today.

Another unintended consequence of the Reformers' efforts to put the Bible into the hands of the common people arose from rapid distribution (thanks to the recently invented printing press) of the most popular translation of all time: the King James Version (KJV) of 1611. While the poetic language of the KJV is unparalleled, it has some interpretive problems. Two continue to be troublesome for Christianity into the present. First, the translators relied heavily on the Latin Vulgate to help them understand the Hebrew and Greek originals. Few, if any, of the translators were proficient in Hebrew. This was not so much because it was a "dead" language, as it was because of pervasive prejudice against all things Jewish, which would be ironic if it were not also infuriatingly sad. Second, the translators were told to produce a translation that discredited Puritan beliefs while also supporting the idea that the rulers of Europe, and especially England, were divinely ordained to their positions. They sought to give credence to the notion that an accident of birth determined who would be the supreme ruler of a nation or territory.

The KJV was the official English translation of the Bible for a long time. Some claim that the 1611 text is the only inspired English translation and therefore carries with it the same authority as the original texts.[19] The naïveté of this is demonstrated by the belief among the literal minded that the words of Jesus as recorded in the KJV are the exact words he spoke. First, reason dictates that Jesus spoke Aramaic, not seventeenth century English. Second, the words of Jesus were recorded in Greek, meaning that what we have is a translation of what he said, not a verbatim account. We do not have the exact words, which does not make the translations unreliable. We can trust that those who wrote down the words of Jesus as recalled by his followers were fluent in the necessary languages and made the most accurate translation possible. There are few significant variations between the many full and fragmentary Greek manuscripts of the Gospels still in existence today, which tells us that the earliest faith communities quickly reached a consensus on the correct translations of Jesus' words. This means that the Gospels accounts are only one language removed from the original. The good news is that, while helpful, learning to read Greek and Hebrew is not an absolute necessity. It is possible to achieve at least a cursory understanding of what Jesus' words mean by embarking on a study of Jewish thought and belief in his time. This is no longer as difficult as it was in the past. Many books have been written that clearly

19. Check it out: https://en.wikipedia.org/wiki/King_James_Only_movement.

describe the religious context that informed Jesus' preaching and teaching. Among these are several books by the late Geza Vermes.

My experience as a teacher of the Bible for almost three decades has convinced me that far too many Christians lack the education, knowledge, and discernment to understand the Bible. It does not have to be this way; to be fair, is not entirely their fault. The Bible can be read intelligently, seeking meaning rather than doctrine, and with recourse to basic information about the historical and religious context. Yes, people should read the Bible. My point is that people should strive to read the Bible intelligently, looking for spiritual guidance, not comforting slogans or carefully selected verses that can be wielded as weapons. Tools that provide the means to read the Bible with understanding are readily available, not the least of which is sincere prayer seeking guidance. This requires effort, however, and it seems to me that many Christians would rather be told what to believe and spend their time doing something more fun than reading the Bible. This plays right into the hands of unscrupulous leaders who twist the meaning of words and phrases in the Bible to support their own personal agenda, which often as not involves controlling others in the name of saving their souls.

The unintended consequences that resulted from decisions made by the early church and the Reformers continue to have an impact. Some translations of the Bible are invested with authority beyond what they deserve, especially those that bear the name of popular authors, pastors, and professors. Biblical scholars deliberately twist Scripture to support their personal agenda, dismissing whatever counters their presuppositions as faulty, not part of the original, or the work of an editor. Couple this with ignorance of the Bible, or at least its historical context, among many Christians today, and you have a recipe for disaster. Knowledge is power, but what we call knowledge these days is subject to all kinds of corruption. The institutional church is dying largely because its members would rather believe what affirms their preferred lifestyle and allows them to pay lip service to their faith than accept the challenge to live faithfully regardless of the personal cost. This is called hypocrisy, and it is killing the church.

Chapter 7

Hypocrisy, Thy Name Is Legion

> We are all hypocrites. We cannot see ourselves or judge ourselves
> the way we see and judge others.
>
> —José Emilio Pacheco[1]

People sometimes legitimately accuse Jesus followers of hypocrisy. Have you ever been called a hypocrite? It is not pleasant. Charges of hypocrisy fly fast and furiously these days at every level of society (as do charges of racism, anti-Semitism, and the like), but I suspect many people making these accusations are parroting what they hear or read without understanding what it means. Merriam-Webster defines hypocrisy, in part, as "behavior that contradicts what one claims to believe or feel."[2] This may seem obvious but let me give an example: One who believes it is wrong to steal yet steals anyway is a hypocrite. One who believes there is nothing wrong about stealing and steals acts according to his or her convictions and is not hypocrite (but is still guilty of a crime). There are plenty of examples of hypocrisy without our needing to create them where they do not exist. I know that absolutes are out of fashion these days, but I think it is fair to say, absolutely, that everyone has been guilty of hypocrisy. Many of us struggle to avoid it daily, if not hourly or by the minute. Unfortunately, we seem to be far more adept at pointing out the hypocrisy in others than recognizing it in ourselves.

Jesus made ample use of the word hypocrisy to describe the behavior of some, but not all, religious leaders and teachers. Peter, his most famous follower aside from Paul, was no stranger to hypocrisy. He urged those who wanted to live in holiness and faith according to the Way of Jesus to put aside

---

1. https://www.azquotes.com/quote/728399.
2. https://www.merriam-webster.com/dictionary/hypocrisy.

hypocrisy, malice, deceit, envy, and slander.[3] Peter was well-qualified to make this exhortation, having battled hypocrisy throughout his life. Would that all those who claimed to be his successors faithfully followed suit! Even the most respected and revered popes in modern times have come under suspicion of hypocrisy as the extent of the sexual abuse scandals at all levels of the Roman Catholic Church is gradually uncovered. Well-known and well-regarded pastors and teachers across Protestantism have fallen victim to the temptation to believe that they are not bound by the same standards of behavior as others. This has been increasingly true during the past fifty years. It seems that honesty and humility have always been in short supply among the leaders of churches of every shape, size, and denomination, with a few notable exceptions, among them the late Billy Graham.[4] The unfortunate reality is that the rank stench of hypocrisy noticeably fills the pews and pulpits of institutional Christianities of every stripe. It is unfortunate most of all because the world does not fail to take notice and pass judgment, blaming Jesus for the bad behavior of those claiming to be his followers.

Is it deliberate? Do self-identified followers of Jesus willfully and intentionally set out to sully the cause of Christ by shamelessly behaving in ways their faith claims are sinful? The answer to this question is not as simple as may seem. It is easier to see and judge the hypocrisy of others than it is to see and judge our own. It is a matter of self-awareness in the case of the latter and self-absorption in the former. There are times when my behavior is hypocritical, but it is rare for me not to feel guilt almost immediately upon doing something that violates my religious or moral convictions. There is a line to be drawn between hypocritical actions accompanied by guilt and hypocritical actions that result from belief that the restrictions placed on others do not apply to you. The latter would be a fair characterization of clergy at the highest levels of the church in the Middle Ages and the Renaissance. It is still present among clergy today. Sometimes hypocrisy is denied or ignored; sometimes it is deliberate. Something I long suspected was recently confirmed as true when I learned that there are anonymous support groups for pastors who have become atheists or agnostics but keep it a secret because they want to retain their current positions, often having no other marketable skills.

I really do not know which is worse: pastors who preach and teach (probably without much conviction) what they no longer believe or pastors who preach utter nonsense under the guise of enlightened truth. My hope is

---

3. "Therefore, rid yourselves of all malice and all deceit, hypocrisy, envy, and slander of every kind" (1 Pet 2:1, NIV).

4. Some Christians accused him of hypocrisy because of his willingness to associate with U.S. Presidents whose moral integrity was questionable, but he never, as far as I know, condoned their behavior.

that God can still use the former. My experience is that the latter has done far more spiritual harm than good. We seem to have forgotten, at least in the Christianities that place a high value on an educated clergy, that the pulpit is for proclamation, not academic lectures. Most people simply are not going to devote time and energy to learning what Jesus said and taught until they arrive at a deep understanding and appreciation of how much he loves them and what he has done for them. Unfortunately, the temptation to tell people what you think they need to hear instead of what they really need to hear is strong. There is also the strong temptation to tell people what they want to hear to keep the seats full and the money flowing. I empathize with both types of pastors, having experienced repeatedly the temptation to compromise my beliefs and tailor the truth I taught and preached to avoid conflict. When the stench of my hypocrisy began to overwhelm me, I faced the temptation to chuck it all, walk away, and do something else with my life, hopefully as far from organized religion as possible. I wish I could say with complete sincerity that I have avoided both temptations. The truth is that I compromised my beliefs many more times than I can count—in part because of my perception that what I was doing in the pulpit was a waste of time and an exercise in futility. Anyone who has not pastored a church cannot understand the pressures pastors face daily, if not hourly. It is no wonder that so many of us burn out and quit rather than yield to the temptation to sacrifice our souls on the altar of hypocrisy. I have, to my chagrin and relief, joined the ranks of those who have left full-time ministry, although I have not walked away from the church, service, or basic Christian faith.

Just what is "basic Christian faith"? I have pondered that question frequently and have arrived at a possible answer. I keep going back to the basic assertions of Jesus and the early church as recorded in the Scriptures. Pared down to the absolute basics, I find that the essence of the Christian faith is to believe, first, that there is one God, whom Jesus called his Father, that God set Jesus apart as his beloved Son and commissioned him to invite humanity into a personal relationship with him, and that eternal life is a gift we can only claim in and through Jesus. Everything else is little more than doctrinal accretions designed to allow fallible human beings to usurp God's divine right to decide who is worthy of heaven and who is bound for hell. The problem is that those claiming the power to determine the eternal destiny of others sometimes appear less worthy of salvation than those they consign to damnation. It is both ironic and hypocritical that those whose spiritual ancestors fought and died because they refused to worship human beings that the Roman Senate declared to be gods could without any apparent sense of shame purport to know who was worthy to be elevated to the rank of sainthood. I fail to see the difference between praying to a deified emperor and praying to a quasi-deified saint.

> The Ministry of Peace concerns itself with war, the Ministry of Truth with lies, the Ministry of Love with torture and the Ministry of Plenty with starvation. These contradictions are not accidental, nor do they result from ordinary hypocrisy: they are deliberate exercises in doublethink.
>
> —GEORGE ORWELL, *1984*[5]

There is plenty of hypocrisy to go around. It is possible that some of it is unintentional rather than deliberate. Although my evidence is anecdotal rather than empirical, my observation is that when hypocrisy manifests itself in the people in the pews it arises to some degree from the belief that the pastor is responsible for leading a life of sanctity and piety far beyond that of the non-clergy because of his or her calling. The hypocrisy here is the belief that the clergy must live exemplary lives first because of their unique calling and second because it frees the common person from having to follow the rules, or at least the inconvenient ones. I am not making this up; people have sincerely voiced these opinions expecting me to accept them as true and binding, which I begrudgingly did for many years. This attitude *should* be abhorrent to Protestants given the doctrine that all believers are equal, and equally responsible for their actions, before God. The notion that members of the clergy serve as mediators between God and the people, explicit in Roman Catholic doctrine, quickly found its way into Protestant practice in ways the Reformers most assuredly did not intend. The vaunted doctrine of the "Priesthood of all Believers," so crucial to the redefinition of the roles of clergy and laity, did not catch on as completely as they might have hoped.[6] Instead, people continued to rely on the clergy to stay the course morally, ethically, and biblically so that they could get on with life.

This was made clear to me early in my ministry when I made the mistake of doing yard work on a Sunday afternoon because my busy schedule and uncooperative weather had not allowed me to do it earlier. Someone saw me doing this and the church board subsequently informed me that it was inappropriate for me, as a pastor, to work on Sunday because it did not honor the Sabbath. I was not pleased but kept my mouth shut to keep the peace. I was, after all, a newly ordained pastor and anxious to make a

---

5.   https://www.goodreads.com/quotes/60071-the-ministry-of-peace-concerns-itself-with-war-the-ministry.

6.   "The Priesthood of all Believers": the doctrine that every individual has direct access to God without the need for mediation by clergy and that everyone shares responsibility for ministry.

good impression. However, the hypocrisy of their directive became glaringly obvious one Sunday morning when, as I was driving to church, I saw a board member blowing leaves off his driveway. This board member did not show up for church that morning and was, in fact, only periodic in his attendance. His position on the board was due in large part to his status in the community and his family's status in the church. In any case, working pastors do not get to honor the Sabbath command to rest since they spend a fair portion of the day attempting to please their temperamental, demanding flocks, some of whom only honor the Sabbath themselves when it is convenient and does not interfere with other activities.

Was his hypocrisy intentional? I do not know, and in any case, I left that community and church long ago. It was one of the more glaring examples I saw in those days, but it was not the only one. I once had a member of that church make an appointment to see me. He told me that had affirmed to his own satisfaction that his wife no longer recognized him due to either Alzheimer's or dementia and that since he had "provided for his wife's care" by putting her in a nursing facility, he intended to see other women. His point in telling me was not to ask my permission, but to let me know ahead of time so that I would not be surprised. He was not ashamed of his actions; in fact, he seemed to believe there was nothing wrong with what he intended to do. I was young and naïve then and did not say anything, but I suspect that he was already seeing someone and expected me to defend his actions, or at least ignore them. I kept silent because I needed my job. Apparently, adultery is only adultery if the offended spouse is aware of it. I wish I could say that this was an isolated incident, but unfortunately it was not the only time I was expected to look the other way to avoid offending an influential individual or family. This is one reason why so many pastors keep going through the motions even after they have given up on their faith. It is also one reason why the professional clergy class needs to be disbanded and abolished, but I am getting ahead of myself.

Hypocrisy has been leaching the life out of the church at every level for many generations because of the pervasive desire on the part of so many Christians that their faith be comforting, but not convicting. People want religion to be convenient, not an onerous burden to bear. They view the church as an extension of the country club, albeit without the usual amenities. Many people look to the church to do the hard work of morally and ethically shaping their children, a task that typically fails because there is little reinforcement at home. Every church I have served has had parents who dropped their children off for Sunday school and then went out to breakfast, returning to pick them up but never darkening the doors themselves. They treated it like free childcare. Leaders and others made all sort of excuses for this behavior including the statement that "at least we have a chance to make an impact on the children," but this is just smoke in the wind. Children whose faith is not reinforced at home face nearly insurmountable odds against remaining faithful beyond their teen years. The church is just another social service, even for those who claim to be faithful Christians. We want to take Jesus at his word when he said that he "came not to be served but to serve,"[7] but not so that we can follow his example. Instead, we want him, and by extension the church and its clergy, to serve us, giving us everything we want (because we hire and financially compensate them) without asking anything in return. In short, we want to be sheep relying on our shepherd to take care of everything so that all we need to do is fill our bellies and lie in the sun.

Jesus was fond of referring to his followers as his sheep and to himself at their shepherd, an image deeply rooted in the Old Testament. The image is meant to convey a sense of comfort and protection, something that is clearly conveyed in Psalm 23, familiar to so many, thanks to its frequency at funerals.[8] Yet, there is a darker side to the image, perpetuated by a stereotype as old as humanity: Sheep are stupid, helpless, defenseless creatures who would not long survive without the protection of a shepherd. One element of that image is partly correct. Sheep are ill-equipped to defend themselves against large predators like lions and bears. The protection of a shepherd helps preserve the flock, especially the weakest and most vulnerable. The notion that the flock needs a shepherd to protect them became a fundamental principle in the church, leading to dependence on the clergy that fostered the biblical and spiritual ignorance of the "sheep"—the laity. Ignorant people, so the thinking goes, are easier to control. This is certainly easier if the people regard their leaders and their actions as necessary to their overall health and well-being.

Sheep are content to be led if they are safe and their bellies are full. Can the same also be said of us? History frequently portrays humanity as composed of a few who desire to lead and a majority who are content to be led. We claim to want freedom of thought and action, but we really want someone to take care of the details, so we can enjoy life in whatever way we desire. There are those who claim that this is one reason why socialist and communist countries exist. It is sometimes thought to be true in the case of democracies and republics. George Washington believed that people should be free from invasive government control over their lives, but the pragmatic part of his personality knew that only a strong central government could prevent anarchy from within and conquest from without. There was isolated

---

7. "just as the Son of Man did not come to be served, but to serve, and to give his life as a ransom for many" (Matt 20:28, NIV).

8. Full disclosure: this is my "go-to" psalm for funerals and graveside services.

opposition to the formation of a central governing authority, mostly from the privileged class (especially Virginia plantation owners), but most people cared more about making enough money to live, and keeping as much of it out of the hands of the tax collectors as possible, than they did about government control. They chose to ignore what they could not change and did not affect them on a personal level.

What does this mean? Simply this: many people are susceptible to intellectual, emotional, political, moral, ethical, and spiritual laziness. There are exceptions, of course, but there seems to be a tendency to believe whatever makes life easy and comfortable. We vote for whoever promises what we want and that we believe will most benefit us. The rapidly decreasing pool of people seeking a "church home" in our country "shop" for the one that offers the most and best programs, the shortest worship service, and the "best" preaching (which usually means the least challenging and most entertaining). I cringe inwardly whenever people tell me that they are "shopping for a new church." The seeker movement that was popular two decades ago, and is still in vogue in parts of the world, is partly responsible for this attitude. The effort to attract people who have rejected Christianity or have no experience of it leads some church leaders to dumb down the gospel, turn sanctuaries into auditoriums, banish music and liturgy that smells the least bit traditional, and develop programs that offer practical help with little or no commitment. They create excitement and a sense of belonging to something big, but often little else. One problem with this is that people become bored if new reasons to be excited are not forthcoming. This leads the people who are not invested in the institution to seek greener pastures elsewhere. Churches find themselves regularly trading members as people wander from one to the next looking for the newest, most exciting programs. If religion has become just another product in our culture, then we have a problem. If religion is just another commodity, then whatever it offers becomes a commodity as well, or more properly a collection of commodities in slightly different packages. Anyone who thinks that finding the right "religious experience" can assure themselves of a comfortable life in the present and eternity in heaven is sadly mistaken.

> Avoid those who seek friends in order to maintain a certain social status or to open doors they would not otherwise be able to approach.
>
> —PAULO COELHO[9]

---

9. https://www.goodreads.com/quotes/1329920-avoid-those-who-seek-friends-in-order-to-maintain-a.

Many churches have become little more than social clubs made up of homogenous collections of people from similar ethnic backgrounds and of similar social status. A generation or two ago it was not uncommon for people to join churches based on their position in the community rather than the doctrine of the church. I heard more than once of people who visited one of the churches I served and enjoyed the worship service, but reluctantly decided that it was not the church for them because they could not afford to go there (based on the clothes people wore and the luxury cars in the parking lot). It would be easy to dismiss this as a modern conceit, but it has been around from the beginning. Once the followers of Jesus began gaining converts and forming communities in Greek-speaking Asia Minor, social elitism reared its head and caused divisions among believers. This happened even though Paul clearly and unambiguously declared that among followers of Jesus "There is neither Jew nor Greek, there is neither slave nor free, there is no male or female."[10] These divisions survived the demise of those early communities and continued traveling west, spreading, growing, and flourishing like a disease that can be managed (barely), but not cured. If you have any doubt about this, look around you the next time you find yourself in church. Homogeneity is the order of the day in most mainline Christian churches. To be fair, this has been true for a long time. The main problem is that it runs counter to every Christian impulse toward inclusiveness. It is trendy for churches (especially liberal and progressing ones) to promote inclusivity as a spiritual value, but their brand of inclusiveness excludes anyone who does not conform to their definition of inclusive. How is that for Orwellian? Inclusivity across economic, social, and racial boundaries is far more important than concerns about sexual preference and gender identity. These kinds of concerns are not invalid, to be sure, but they should not be what drives the impulse to invite people of every type into the fellowship of Jesus followers.

Social and economic divisions get in the way of Christian unity when they are transplanted into the church. There is nothing inherently wrong with wealth in and of itself. It is not money, but the *love* of money that is the root of all kinds of evil.[11] This creates divisions. Money represents power and security in every culture and at every time in history. As such, it is a source of temptation in all areas of life. Those who have money want to keep it as often as not, and usually want to accumulate more of it. They tend to

10. There is neither Jew nor Gentile, neither slave nor free, nor is there male and female, for you are all one in Christ Jesus (Gal 3:28, NIV).

11. For the love of money is a root of all kinds of evils. It is through this craving that some have wandered away from the faith and pierced themselves with many pangs (1 Tim 6:10, ESV).

form meaningful social connections primarily with those in their own economic class. This can be awkward when their children form relationships with peers in lower classes, especially when those relationships result in marriage. Perception is often far more important than reality, and the perceptions that rich and poor typically have of one another tends to trump reality. Those who have money often cannot understand why those with fewer resources are jealous. Those who do not have money often resent the rich for their wealth and privilege. The problem is that this creates divisions in churches that hinder effective ministry. This is not new. Jesus had a lot to say about money and the problems and dangers associated with possessing or desiring it. Many of his followers through the centuries chose to finesse his words to support their financial practices and attitudes, especially regarding how much money churches and pastors should possess. Just as pastors seek it to further their agendas by catering to the affluent members of a church, so some of the wealthy use it, consciously or unconsciously, to influence or gain control of that agenda. Why do some Christians put wealth, power, and prestige ahead of following in the Way of Jesus?

Many Christians in the United States express their faith in terms of what they can get from it, not what they can contribute to it. The comment that "I didn't get anything out of the sermon" prompts me to wonder what that person brought to the experience. Did they want to be entertained or to have their own views confirmed? I was once publicly taken to task by someone following a sermon for daring to express an opinion that did not match her liberal views. She told me that she "didn't come to church to hear that sort of thing." I was speechless at the time, being intimidated by her anger, but repaid her with courtesy and goodwill whenever she was in church until she finally moved on to another congregation more to her liking. This was only one instance among many in my time as a pastor. It has become clear to me that people want to be entertained whenever they decide to make time to come to church, which I always knew but did not want to accept. They certainly do not want to be challenged, unless the challenge is so abstract that there is no way to meet it. The best comment a pastor can receive after a sermon is not "Great sermon pastor!" but "That really convicted me."[12] Unfortunately, few people want to be reminded that their lives do not reflect true devotion to Jesus. They tend to feel bad in the moment, but soon forget the discomfort and move on to more enjoyable activities. A blessed few, however, take it to heart and try to better themselves spiritually.

12. The second comment was said to me a fair number of times in the last church I served.

The hypocrisy in the institutional church, in both leaders and followers, has as much to do with church structure and government as it does with theology. The perpetuation and preservation of the institution is deemed (consciously or unconsciously) to be more important than the proclamation of the gospel. When this happens, it means that the institution is no longer serving Jesus. The church does not need to be an institution with a bureaucracy, hierarchy, or autocratic leader because it already has the best and only leader it needs—Jesus. When Jesus declared to Peter that he was the rock upon which the faith-community would be built, he was referring to Peter's declaration that Jesus was the Messiah, not the person of Peter and those who would succeed him. The Papacy has done far more to harm the cause of Christ up to this point in history than it has done to help because of this focus on who should rule the church. It boils down to the desire to control others and have power over them. Protestants have not done any better, creating institutions that rival Catholicism in their attempts to impose their views upon the faithful.

> Immorality is the word we use to describe people that are not sinning the same way we are.
>
> —SHANNON L. ALDER[13]

Hypocrisy is a scourge upon the church because it so obvious to outsiders and so tempting for the church to deny it. The rank stench of hypocrisy billows forth from churches all along the theological spectrum. Churches that claim to be "welcoming and affirming" only welcome and affirm those who embrace their views on ethics and morality and support of progressive/liberal social justice causes. At the other end of the spectrum, churches ardently claiming to be "Bible-based" actively recruit those who read the "correct" Bible translations and fit into their socio-economic demographic. Heaven forbid that someone show up wearing the wrong clothes or from the wrong side of town! Churches of every stripe loudly trumpet adherence to biblical values but pick and choose the values to which they want to be faithful, rejecting any that do not fit into their preferred standard of behavior as irrelevant in the modern age or that they believe are superseded by Jesus' statements about love (as they define them). The values they reject are most often those that make the church distinct from the world, which is a slippery slope indeed. Embracing the latest fads may win some fans but will not ultimately help the institutional church because it entails rejecting

---

13. "Quotes by Shannon L. Alder." *September 2013* (blog), *lds ponderings*, September 23, 2013, https://ldsponderings.wordpress.com/2013/09/23/wise-words-from-shannon-l-alder-a-mazing.

the validity of significant portions of the document that stands at the heart of the Christian faith. It is akin to a retail establishment opening its doors and allowing its customers to set whatever price they deem fair for the items they are selling. How long would such a store last?

Liberal/progressive institutional Christianities are dying because they profess belief in a risen Lord while declaring that he might not have existed, that his resurrection was only symbolic and that his "lordship" is only valid over those areas of life they want to yield to him. The lie of progressivism is that Jesus is not Lord over any act placed within the context of tolerance or love, according to the current definition of the terms. Is it coincidental that the number of young people identifying as transgender, bisexual, homosexual, asexual, and pansexual has skyrocketed in direct proportion to the vocal support of our society? The suicides rate is disproportionally high among these groups. Reasons vary, as they do for suicides among the general population, but one reason is a sense of rejection. Institutional Christianity has dropped the ball. One extreme condemns such individuals to eternal damnation for their actions. The other extreme lauds them for their bravery. Both extremes need to focus on helping people learn to look beyond themselves and concentrate on reaching out to others with compassion.

On the other end of the spectrum, the most conservative/fundamentalist churches stridently declare that every word in the Bible must be taken literally but lift those words out of context to support all kinds of bizarre beliefs and doctrines, not the least of which is that the primary purpose of prayer is to make one healthy and prosperous. They vociferously assert that homosexuals are destined for hell, even though, if they truly take the Bible literally, Jesus is the only one with the authority to make that judgment. They bring disrepute upon the church because they come across as ignorant, intolerant, and judgmental. Their motives may be sincere, but their methods leave much to be desired. The threat of eternal damnation no longer means anything to people who, if they believe in a life after death at all, believe that everyone goes to their personal version of heaven when they die. The promise of eternal life only means something to those who hold onto the hope that something better awaits them after death. Religion in general, and institutional Christianity in particular, no longer seems willing or able to offer a cogent, coherent assessment of what awaits us after death or what we need to do, if anything, to get to the right place. Assurance of a place in heaven starts with a relationship, not a change in behavior. The change in behavior is the result of the relationship, not its cause.

Institutional Christianity in the West is dying because it is no longer relevant. It is no longer relevant because it is no longer distinctive, having hypocritically declared the need to be "in the world but not of it" while simultaneously adopting corporate models of governance, large support staffs, vision, mission, and purpose statements, and institutional nomenclature. The avalanche of paper flowing out of many churches is a poor example of stewardship of resources as well as a waste of money. Pastor and staff are pummeled with paperwork, tied to their desks, and forced to prioritize tasks that have no eternal significance—all in the name of maintaining an institution allegedly focused on helping people grow spiritually. It is no wonder that Jesus' simple message is being drowned out. There is a message to be shared, one that has the power to transform people. Unfortunately, the relentless pressure to conform to the morally ambiguous and ethically confused assertions of society have browbeaten many otherwise faithful followers of Jesus into silence and submission. The result is that institutional Christianity is no longer growing; on the contrary—it is dying. Tragically, it is fighting for survival even as it retreats from the front lines of the battle, wasting resources that could be put to better use helping the hurting and reaching the lost instead of propping up and supporting an institution that is terminally ill. I believe that Christianity is overdue for reformation, but not one that only goes halfway like the last one. In truth, what is needed is not a reformation, but a revolution that will transform the church into what Jesus wanted it to be, separating it from institutionalism, a professional clergy, opulent campuses, and worldly prestige. The hypocrisies of institutional Christianity in the Western world are legion for at least two reasons. First, it is impossible to proclaim the gospel with integrity while espousing secular values, beliefs, and practices. Second, the church, such as it is, has become just one more institution in a world filled with them. The church does not need reform as much as it needs purification. Radical words, to be sure, and I am certainly not the first Christian to utter them. Most of those who did so in the past ended up imprisoned or dying as martyrs. So be it. The church needs to jettison the baggage that has held it back and step into the future boldly with faith and fervency for what really matters, which means that the church as we know it needs to die so that a new reality can be born.

Chapter 8

Ignorance Is Only Bliss
If You Could Not Care Less

> You are not entitled to your opinion. You are entitled to your *informed* opinion. No one is entitled to be ignorant.
>
> —Harlan Ellison[1]

It is said that laughter is good for the soul and I believe it. I enjoy laughing. Some people find my laughter annoying; others find it contagious. I will admit that there have been times when my attempts to find the humor in situations were not well received. This has been especially true in my Bible teaching. There is plenty of humor in the Bible, but it is invisible to those who insist on idolizing the text instead of trying to learn from it. There are those who hold the opinion that humor has no place in the Bible, or even in discussions about the Bible. I disagree. The stories in the Bible are designed to teach lessons; some do so with humor. This is perfectly natural when we realize that the stories that were eventually written down and collected into what we now know as the Hebrew Scriptures were born and grew up in an oral culture, which is one reason why many of the stories are narratives. They were lovingly and carefully crafted to be remembered, told around the campfire, and faithfully passed on to future generations. Why should they not also be humorous? The failure to discern moments of humor in the Bible has resulted in some silly arguments, one of which being that Jesus never laughed or demonstrated any amusement. I hope and believe that God has a sense of humor. Jesus laughed, when he was not driven to tears by the stubborn stupidity of the people around him.

---

1. https://www.brainyquote.com/quotes/harlan_ellison_922874.

Churches can be depressing places. The one place where joy is supposed to be abundant is sometimes shrouded in the depressing shadows of darkness and gloom. There are many reasons for this, to be sure, but one of them is that far too many followers of Jesus take themselves far too seriously. Christians at both ends of the ideological spectrum wallow in gloominess and anger even as they solemnly profess joy in Jesus. Progressives proudly claim freedom from the constraints of the backward thinking of their spiritual ancestors, but cannot help being persistently angry at those benighted, ignorant, conservative church members who do not subscribe to their enlightened way of thinking about the Bible and faith. Conservatives and evangelicals alike cling to their ancient creeds and beliefs without making any real effort to understand what they mean or how they came to be, viewing with pity and anger those who wantonly abandon traditional doctrines. Those in the middle dwell in an immense cloud of doubt and anger without really understanding it, although they unconsciously sense it. Ignorance is *not* bliss! Who knew? People become disillusioned by the all-too-human nature of church-going folk and quietly walk away from organized religion, often not really knowing why, but sure that there must be something better and more fulfilling out there, somewhere. Pastors also walk away from active participation in organized religion, but rarely with any sense of joy. Most of us are exhausted by the constant, relentless pressure to conform and compromise in the name of helping the institution attract new members, preferably ones with plenty of liquid assets they can contribute to the latest cause or building campaign.

Pastors all too easily fall into the trap of contributing to the biblical and/spiritual ignorance of the people in the pews. I respectfully submit that this situation is at least partly fostered by the prevailing notion that clergy are educated professionals. Some of them clearly want to be viewed this way, deliberately setting out to conform their ministry to current business models, using the latest technology, and insisting on having all their credentials listed every time their names are in print. I confess that I resist being referred to as "reverend" because it fosters the impression that I am better than the average Christian, which is far from true. My formal education has long since been eclipsed by what I have learned while serving as a pastor. Unfortunately, this does not mean much in the eyes of the professional clergy, especially since I did not attend a prestigious seminary or study under well-known scholars and have no interest in earning a doctorate. Education *is* good and beneficial. Mainline denominations rightly require those seeking ordination to attend seminary and/or gain a basic level of proficiency in biblical interpretation, sermon preparation, and doctrine. But seminaries can be spiritually dangerous places if for no other reason than that they contribute to the notion that clergy are a cut above the people they lead, which is pervasive, but patently untrue. Unfortunately, people in the pews contribute to this when they insist that only pastors are qualified to teach the Bible to adults (not incidentally freeing them from the responsibility). My experience is that some pastors support this notion because it gives them the power to promote their interpretation of Scripture as the only valid one. I suspect that some pastors learned how to do this during their seminary training. It is to my lasting shame and regret that I resisted training people to teach the Bible to adults because I enjoyed the praise and adulation I received and because I was afraid that people would not respond well to being taught by someone who was not perceived to be an "expert" on the Bible. I was afraid that no one would be able to teach the Bible with the level of understanding and knowledge I brought to the task. In short, I believed that my way of approaching the Bible was the best and only way.

College education seems to be designed to create the impression that there is one correct way to view reality. This is not new. It may not be as prevalent in some institutions of higher learning as it is in others, but pressure was immediately brought to bear when I began my Protestant seminary education to conform to specific ways of thinking and speaking in public. It was a punishable offense to submit papers or other academic work that did not use inclusive language to refer to people. Bonus points were awarded to those who carried this over into language referring to God. While this may have well-served those students who ended up in large liberal churches, it did not help those of us (the majority) who landed in small conservative churches and communities across the Midwest. Naturally, we were told that it was our duty to enlighten the poor benighted masses placed in our care and drag them, kicking and screaming if necessary, into the modern world. What really happened was that most those who refused to conform to the linguistic, doctrinal, and theological expectations of our churches were crucified. Another reason the institutional church is dying is because those at the top of the hierarchical food chain assume and demand that people bow to their superior knowledge and do what they are told. Ignorance is useful when it allows the educated to control what the masses think and believe, but it is not bliss.

In any case, the deficits in my training because of a bias toward large churches meant that I was ill-prepared to serve in small churches, which were the only positions open to me upon graduation. One reason was that I did not come from a prestigious church or seminary and refused to play politics to get ahead. Since my degree was from a seminary judged to be liberal and academically sub-par by many churches in the denomination, my search for a job was limited to a specific geographical area in the Midwest or to places that were desperate for pastors. My options were limited, but I did not doubt that God was in charge. Thus, I began my ministry in a small struggling church in southwest Indiana. It was good place to start pastoral ministry and to begin a family, but not without its problems. I left on good terms after five years, believing that I had accomplished what God sent me there to do. Above all, I will never forget how the people there welcomed me, my wife, and our newborn daughter with open arms, serving as surrogate parents and grandparents in the absence of our families, who were hundreds of miles away. They were the textbook definition of what it means to be a family church.

My next call was to a smaller church in a smaller community in central Ohio. It was a difficult experience. After four years I reached the conclusion that I was not cut out for ministry as a solo pastor, and maybe not even cut out for ministry at all and sought a position as an associate pastor. One came my way and I traveled to a larger church in central Illinois where I served more than seventeen years under four different pastors. During my time there I was pressured to criticize or oppose the head pastor. I also served temporarily as head pastor several times. I strove not to take sides or be dragged into a struggle for power. I was not head pastor material. Although I strongly considered it during my thirty months acting as Interim Head of Staff, my experience confirmed my belief that I lacked the qualifications, skills, and drive to be the head pastor of a multi-staff institutional church. During the times when I had to pilot the ship, I tried to keep my head down and my mouth shut, doing what I could to hold everyone together as the congregation experienced one transition after another. For the most part I pretended ignorance to keep my sanity but failed in the end and almost gave up on my faith and my call to ministry as a result.

> The strain of anti-intellectualism has been a constant thread winding its way through our political and cultural life, nurtured by the false notion that democracy means that "my ignorance is just as good as your knowledge."
>
> —ISAAC ASIMOV[2]

Ignorance is a double-edged sword. If one edge is bliss, then the other edge can best be described as apathy. The leaders of the Protestant Reformation believed that ignorance was killing the church and hampering the efforts of the faithful to live according to the gospel. Their belief was that the faithful were ignorant not because they had no desire to learn, but because the church forbade common people from reading the Bible in any

---

2. https://www.azquotes.com/quote/605076.

language except Latin. I believe that the Reformers were sincere in their desire to remedy the situation. I also believe that their zeal blinded them to the spiritual and intellectual apathy that was the real reason for much of the ignorance among followers of Jesus. Christians in our own time may know more (or have access to more knowledge) than their religious ancestors, but the willingness to move beyond the most basic of beliefs requires more effort and attention that many seem to want to devote to it. They believe that ignorance is not really ignorance; it is an alternate form of equally valid knowledge. In any case, many do not want to do anything about it because it would take intellectual effort. People tend to find social media much more interesting and engaging—and certainly far less challenging. Some claim that it is a great tool for spreading the gospel, but most of what I see of a spiritual or religious nature on social media is innocuous. Some is so heretical that the authors would have been imprisoned or executed in less permissive times.

Ignorance and apathy are part of the reason why the average believer allows the hierarchy of the church to make itself the sole arbiter of biblical interpretation, and by extension, salvation, thereby making the church a spiritual autocrat in matters of faith and practice. Simply put: The Roman Catholic Church until recent times claimed that it alone possessed the keys to heaven and hell, with the pope being the ultimate authority to determine who ended up in which place. It should be noted that arguments about the validity of this statement rarely descended from the halls of academia into the hearts and homes of most European Christians.[3] Monarchs, theologians, nobles, and academicians had the education and the time to debate the finer points of doctrine and biblical interpretation. On the other hand, most people living in Europe in the fifth to the mid-sixteenth centuries were wholly occupied with scratching out a living and devising ways to keep as much as possible out of the hands of the tax collectors (who worked as often for the church as for the secular government). War was an ever-present fact of life, impoverishing the populace, driving them into starvation, depriving them of their possessions, and often murdering them. At the same time, people in that supposedly benighted age generally had a better grasp of doctrine and theology than do Christians in the enlightened present. They were simply incapable, given the intertwining of religion and government, of doing anything to change their circumstances. The best course of action

---

3. In all fairness, the Eastern Churches were no better in this regard. The biggest difference was that most Orthodox Churches were firmly under the control of the autocrats in whose dominions they operated and therefore limited as to how much they could influence doctrine and belief.

was to keep one's head down, try not to attract too much attention from the authorities, and save the theological discussions for the pub.

Let me be clear: I do not blame the average person living in Europe in those perilous times for not wanting to devote much time to anything beyond casual discussions about spiritual or theological matters; they had all they could do simply to survive. Jesus declared that there will always be poor people,[4] which is why he taught a simple message that did not require advanced theological degrees or training to understand. There is doctrine, and then there is practice. When doctrine replaces practice as the primary concern of faith, salvation becomes focused on knowledge instead of action. It shifts from belief in a person (Jesus) for salvation to belief in a set of doctrines. This was true of Jesus' religion in his day. He did much to simplify the meaning of faithfulness to better inculcate it in the hearts and minds of ordinary people. Unfortunately, those at the highest levels of society and the church took it upon themselves to interpret and expand upon what Jesus said for the benefit of the poor and ignorant masses to fit their own interpretation. Their biggest mistake was making salvation dependent upon belief in the right doctrine instead of belief in the right person. This began happening as soon as Judaism started barring followers of Jesus from the synagogue and consequently pushing Christians toward Greek philosophy. Given human nature, it is only natural that this led in turn to Christian leaders and rulers blaming Jews solely for the death of Christ, a position they held more out of spite than anything else. Ignorance is relative, being dependent on how one defines knowledge, understanding, and intelligence.

> There are two ways to be fooled. One is to believe what isn't true; the other is to refuse to believe what is true.
>
> —SØREN KIERKEGAARD[5]

I find it both fascinating and frustrating that anyone with a lot of money is automatically assumed to be intelligent. The perception that the wealthy are intrinsically better than the poor allowed many of the rich and powerful of the world over the centuries to set themselves above those who are less affluent socially, economically, and even spiritually. Taking away their wealth and giving it to others is not the answer because that would only change the dynamic, not solve the problem. Poverty is real but must never be used as an excuse for oppression or condescension. Whatever you may think of the legal code in the Hebrew Scriptures, clear provisions were

---

4. "For you always have the poor with you, but you will not always have me" (Matt 26:11, ESV).

5. https://www.azquotes.com/quote/353575.

made for the care of the poor that did not rely on government intervention. People were supposed to take care of one another as a matter of faith. In fact, when the Israelites demanded a monarchy, one of God's prophets warned them that it would cause more problems than it solved because the king would take what they had earned by the sweat of their brows and give it to others who had not worked for it.[6] Jesus intended that his followers be counter-cultural, which means that in embracing cultural structures, values, and practices built upon the premise that financial prosperity is a sign of divine blessing, all the while claiming to be carrying on his mission, the church is engaged in hypocrisy. It is tempting to blame it on ignorance, but I am not so sure that is the case.

I often wonder why it is that regardless of the form of the government—monarchy, theocracy, democracy, autocracy, socialism, or communism—societies invariably end up with a relatively small, wealthy, powerful class ruling over an impoverished, powerless majority. Is it a question of ignorance? Is it a subconscious refusal to see the truth? The problem, at least for the ruling class, is that even the most ignorant and self-deluded people are eventually goaded by their circumstances to rise from their slumber and violently wield the only useful weapon available to them: revolution. It takes different forms and results in different outcomes, but the "successful" ones bring change, if not always for the better. Napoleon Bonaparte is labeled a tyrant by many historians but significant elements of his efforts at civil and governmental reform are still in use around the world today. The Socialist movement following the Russian Revolution and the rise of unionism in the United States, prior to its entry into World War I, sought both better pay and conditions for workers, allegedly to improve their living conditions. The means and results were different, to say the least.[7] Neither completely solved the problems, as evidenced by the subsequent Great Depression in America and Stalinism in what became the U.S.S.R. However, both made contributions to society and culture that are still in place today.

People are effectively stirred to action when impacted by something. Even then, they will usually only act when it affects them directly. Otherwise, they look to those in authority to lead the charge. Ignorance is bliss, or so the saying goes. Read some of the opinions expressed against America's entry into World War I and you will see the truth of this statement. Opponents decried that American involvement in a European conflict would only benefit the wealthy at the cost of the blood of hardworking, poor Americans

---

6. Read 1 Sam 8:11–18. Do the warnings seem familiar?

7. Interestingly, 1917 (four hundred years after the Protestant Reformation) was a pivotal year for both these movements.

who wanted nothing more than to live their lives in peace. It is not unreasonable to conclude that war has consistently drained every nation of its best and brightest people, notwithstanding assertions on the part of some that the only people who enlist in the armed services are those who are unqualified for anything else. The reasons for armed conflicts between nations can be simple, but even the simplest reason generally stands on the shoulders of a complex series of sometimes seemingly unrelated circumstances.

It is tempting to accept the easy (though not entirely accurate) answer than to do the difficult work of uncovering the hard but more precise one. This is as true of institutional Christianities as it is of the cultures in which they live and work. For instance, it is easy to say that followers of Jesus are supposed to love one another, but uncovering and accepting what that means can be hard, mostly because we do not like what it requires of us in a practical sense. Ignorant people following ignorant pastors teaching an ignorant interpretation of the Bible have done and continue to do much damage—in ignorance. To be fair, clever people following clever pastors teaching a clever interpretation of the Bible do not fare much better. The most dangerous form of ignorance is the one that results from lazy acceptance of easy truth. It is dangerous because it so often goes unrecognized and unacknowledged. The antidote to ignorance is education, as many have opined over the centuries, but not just any kind of education. Incontrovertible facts in the arena of religious belief are few given the nature of faith. We need to hold tightly to the most basic assertions of faith and hold lightly to doctrinal statements developed centuries after the life and death of Jesus. Attempts at uncovering the facts must be limited to verifiable data, as is also true in the scientific world. Everything else belongs to the realm of faith, which cannot, by nature, be empirically proven. This does not mean, however, that religious faith and secular education are incompatible.

> We are all born ignorant, but one must work hard to remain stupid.
>
> —BENJAMIN FRANKLIN[8]

The leaders of the Reformation believed that putting the Bible into the hands of the people was the key to unlocking the chains of ignorance that bound the faithful to blind obedience to the church. The Reformation was an educated movement with a dose of good old-fashioned rebellion thrown in. It was sparked by a desire for intellectual debate on specific matters of theology and doctrine—matters that could only be understood through study, which required the ability to read. The time needed to learn to read was a

8. https://www.azquotes.com/quote/364616.

luxury few could afford, let alone the fact that the precious hours of daylight were better utilized for tasks more essential to life on this side of eternity. The average person necessarily relied on a supposedly educated clergy to tell them how to act and what to believe. The clergy did little to alleviate this, jealously guarding the authority to dictate correct belief and doctrine, which meant the doctrines and beliefs most useful to the support of institutional Christianity. Gradually, perhaps unconsciously, the essential tenet that the way to get to heaven was by belief in and relationship to a person shifted to belief in and acceptance of a set of doctrines. The Reformation succeeded in putting the Bible into the hands of the faithful, but it did not do as well in helping them understand Jesus' message. This is one reason the Reformation spawned so many other reformation movements. Once freed from the tyranny of doctrines imposed without clear explanation, educated people throughout Europe began to question *every* biblical and doctrinal authority.

The sincere efforts of the Reformers to eliminate meaningless rules resulted, perhaps unintentionally, in more rules, leading to the rise of fundamentalism and the proliferation of multiple institutional Christianities claiming to be the true successors to Jesus' mission. I liken the Reformation to chemotherapy: While it often kills the cancer, it also kills healthy cells in the body and can be worse than the disease. The Reformation killed the doctrinal and financial stranglehold the Roman Catholic Church held on Europe but created a new cancer in the process: institutional Christianities. The notion that the church could exist as a national entity apart from Catholicism was a product of the nearly parallel development of Lutheranism[9] in Germany and Anglicanism in England.[10] Once the initial break was made, denominationalism spread like an uncontrollable, inoperable cancer throughout Europe and then into the New World. This is not to say that the impulse to institutionally enforce doctrine disappeared. It was constantly challenged, but every subsequent movement that dared to reject institutionalism in any form and the attendant emphasis on uniformity of doctrine either compromised or died.

Successful revolutions/reformations were led, or at least guided by, those who had the time and energy to devote to it. The inchoate masses may have been dissatisfied with their lot, but most believed they were powerless to change their circumstances. In any case, when they did rebel it usually focused on minutia rather than critical issues. In the religious arena, my experience over the last three decades has shown me that most people care

9. Luther hated that label, by the way.

10. It should be noted that no precedent was being set here. The Eastern Orthodox Church, based in Constantinople, and the Roman Catholic Church had long been separate entities by this time.

more about ritual, superstition, and habit than correct doctrine, belief, or practice. Publicly question the validity of certain passages in the Bible and many Christians will shrug their shoulders and complain about the quality of the coffee and donuts at the fellowship hour. Ignorance is bliss for them because it means not having to engage with the Bible and change comfortable and enjoyable beliefs and behaviors. By contrast, suggest changing the style of music, order of worship, wording of a prayer, or the color of the carpet and you will start World War III in the church. People would rather argue about money (something they understand) than doctrine (something they are reluctant to understand) My perception is that people are content to rely on others to tell them what to believe and only object when it threatens to significantly interfere with their lifestyle. Reformation, when it finally happens, is usually driven by church leaders, supposedly for the benefit of believers. While it is ostensibly driven by doctrine, the actual issues are money, authority, and power.

> The hardest thing to explain is the glaringly evident which everybody has decided not to see.
>
> —AYN RAND[11]

I speak from personal experience. I re-surrendered to God's persistent, inescapable call to serve him in the ministry in 1988 when I abandoned my call to be a priest in the Roman Catholic Church and joined the Presbyterian Church (USA). It was a relatively new denomination, having formed when Presbyterians who divided prior to the Civil War agreed to merge in 1983, resulting in a moderately liberal denomination, although I was unaware of this at the time. I attended what was described as a liberal seminary and spent the first decade of my ministry serving small rural churches in the Midwest. Over the next two decades the leadership of the denomination moved gradually but persistently in a direction that did not sit well with the members of many conservative churches, including those I served. In response, seven pastors of some of the largest churches in the denomination began a movement in 2010 to organize a response. This resulted in the formation of a new Presbyterian denomination a few years later. Although it takes pains to characterize itself as a movement and works to promote the health of the individual church over the organization, it retains enough of the structure it left behind to put it in danger of following the same path.[12] In fact, an uncomfortable percentage of those who led the revolution (and

---

11. https://www.brainyquote.com/quotes/ayn_rand_386180.

12. Including, unfortunately, the use of incomprehensible acronyms to identify committees.

their spouses) now serve in leadership positions in the movement. I sincerely hope I am wrong, but it appears that this new denomination will follow the path of its institutional predecessors.

As much as I approve of this movement, what we need is a radical revolution, not a quiet reformation. But we will never have one so long as the average Christian does not care about learning and living the gospel and actively sharing it with others. The biggest enemies of faith are ignorance and apathy, and there is plenty to go around at every level of the institution. The average Christian cares more about convenient charity work, keeping up with the neighbors economically, and popular social activism than learning what it means to bear and declare the message of eternal life. The movement to force institutional Christianity into a form more acceptable to our permissive, sex-obsessed, self-destructive, morally confused culture will destroy the very thing it claims to want to reform. The parts of institutional Christianity that becomes indistinguishable from the culture will vanish into obscurity. I am willing to say a few words at the funeral, free of charge by the way. It is the least I can do.

I wonder why so many Christians remain woefully ignorant about what the Bible says and teaches. Is it deliberate, or is it just laziness? I fear the former and suspect the latter. Jesus accused some of his opponents of "straining out a gnat and swallowing a camel."[13] He meant by this that they were quibbling over minutiae and non-essentials while ignoring the larger principles of faith and belief. We desperately work to believe the lies that bring us comfort while ignoring the truths that offends us or, perhaps more importantly, make us unpopular with our family and friends. I have seen far too many examples of this, most recently in efforts to force Christianity to endorse all kinds of sexual behavior as morally acceptable. This is what the apostle Paul called exchanging the truth for a lie.[14] Let me be clear: In stating that sexual behavior outside the context of marriage between one man and one woman is wrong I am not declaring that anyone who engages in these behaviors is bound for hell. The problem is that a minority have managed to convince the majority that love is just a feeling or an emotion, one that allows for every kind of sexual behavior, even those once regarded as deviant by most of society (with the exception, so far, of pedophilia). There are multiple problems with this position. People who think and believe this way worship a permissive, passive, non-judgmental Jesus. That is not the

13. "You blind guides! You strain out a gnat but swallow a camel!" (Matt 23:24).

14. "Therefore, God gave them up in the lusts of their hearts to impurity, to the degrading of their bodies among themselves, because they exchanged the truth about God for a lie and worshiped and served the creature rather than the Creator, who is blessed forever! Amen" (Rom 1:24–25).

Jesus we meet in the Bible. Jesus consistently showed compassion and offered healing to anyone suffering from oppressive sin or illness. This was
not to say that he condoned sin; but that he saw it as an illness that could be
cured, not something that should be affirmed because it is too hard or too
inconvenient to change.

Institutional Christianity is being browbeaten into submission by
elements in our culture that, if they do not seek its outright destruction,
demand its complicity in the complete destruction of traditional values. The
institution goes along with it because, more than anything else, it wants to
survive as an institution. Like Adam and Eve in the garden of Eden, institutional Christianity has accepted as true the lie of the serpent: God's love is
permissive, not prohibitive. In other words, if God loves you, he will let you
do whatever you want without consequence. The reality, on the contrary, is
that love sets boundaries on relationships because nature sets boundaries on
what is proper, healthy, and fulfilling. Ignorance allows the devil to convince
us otherwise. The shameful, undeniable truth is that institutional Christianity is complicit in the destruction of the moral fabric of society. I have
shared in this, but no more. Reformation is not enough. The last tepid reformation in which I participated is falling slowly but surely into the trap of
institutionalism. Now is the time for revolution. Christianity belongs in and
to the households and families of the faithful, first and foremost, not in the
vaulted worship centers, hallowed halls, lavish offices, and well-appointed
campuses of institutional Christianity.

This raises an obvious question: Can the Jesus movement survive
without organization and structure? The answer is yes, but only if the
movement fully returns to and then completely sticks to the basics: salvation comes through faith in Jesus followed by a lifestyle that faithfully
follows the path he established. Feed the hungry, clothe the naked, visit
the imprisoned, love your neighbor, and give away everything you do not
need to live. If you own a home that sits empty more than it is occupied,
cars that are in a garage more than they are on the road, and more money
than you need to take care of your needs for the foreseeable future, then
you have too much. This is clearly not consistent with the "American
Dream," but the Jesus movement existed long before the United States of
America was born and will exist long after it is gone. God does not give so
we can have; he gives so we can give. The one who dies with the most toys
still dies, and the toys go to someone else. Institutional Christianity and
those who serve it refuse to make such pronouncements. This is one more
reason for the demise of the institutional church.

Ignorance is not bliss. I know this from experience. Instead, it is one
of the weapons the devil uses in the battle to destroy the Jesus movement.

Ignorance makes us complacent. It keeps us from understanding what is important. It allows us to delude ourselves into believing what is reasonable, comfortable, and acceptable instead of what is true. Ignorance in the church has led to apathy and acquiescence to every lie perpetrated by a world bent on destroying itself in an orgy of self-indulgence and self-destructive pleasure. The demonic pressure placed upon us by such a world demands that we bless what God calls sin in the name of "love." This perverted love leads to destruction. When will the true followers of Jesus rise, throw off the yoke of ignorance, and reclaim the mission he entrusted to us?

Chapter 9

Vanity of Vanities . . . All Is Vanity[1]

When dealing with people, let us remember we are not dealing with creatures of logic. We are dealing with creatures of emotion, creatures bristling with prejudices and motivated by pride and vanity.

—DALE CARNEGIE[2]

Merriam-Webster defines vanity, in part, as "inflated pride in oneself or one's appearance" or "something that is vain, empty, or valueless." A suggested synonym is "conceit."[3] There is a difference between taking pride in one's accomplishments and using them as an excuse to lord it over others. That behavior is annoying when encountered among the rich and famous, but abhorrent when it manifests itself among those who claim to be followers of Jesus. "I have seen everything that is done under the sun," moaned the writer of Ecclesiastes, "and behold, all is vanity and a striving after the wind."[4] If, as tradition holds, the author of those words was King Solomon, then he certainly knew whereof he spoke. He expended vast sums of money building a magnificent palace and an ornate temple that he believed would never be surpassed in grandeur and splendor. Solomon's hopes were in vain, as his remarkable edifice paled in comparison to the one built by one of his successors named Herod centuries later. Not to be outdone by a couple Jews, Justinian (AD 482–565), neo-pagan ruler of the Roman Empire (more Byzantine that Roman), built the Hagia Sophia in Constantinople in AD 537.

1. "Vanity of vanities, says the Teacher, vanity of vanities! All is vanity" (Eccl 1:2).

2. https://www.azquotes.com/quote/48678.

3. https://www.merriam-webster.com/dictionary/vanity.

4. "I saw all the deeds that are done under the sun; and see, all is vanity and a chasing after wind" (Eccl 1:14).

He is reported to have declared "Solomon I have outdone thee" upon entering the basilica for the first time. Justinian's vanity was matched only by his
insecurity. The magnificent church he built to honor "Holy Wisdom," and
ostentatiously dedicated to the Son of God, is now a museum.

Speaking as an active member of the clergy for almost three decades,
I feel qualified to state that the vanity of members of the clergy class, mani-
fested as conceit, pretentiousness and pomposity, is one reason why institutional Christianity is spiraling down the sewer pipe of human history. These
characteristics are not infrequently displayed by the proud graduates of
prestigious seminaries. I did not attend one of those schools. Naïve as I was
at the time, it never occurred to me that there was any difference between
the seminaries of the denomination in which I was ordained. I assumed that
it was a matter of geography than anything else, but soon found that I was
mistaken. It became clear to me during the first decade after I was ordained
that the seminary one attended and the scholars under whom one studied
mattered very much in terms of prestige among one's peers as well as career
advancement. Since I did not attend one of the flagship institutions of higher
learning and could not claim tutelage under one of the revered stars of academia, I could never hope to serve churches in certain parts of the country
or of a certain size. It was not always an issue of liberal verses conservative,
although that was often the case. Pastors typically begin a conversation by
inquiring about the size of their congregation and worship attendance. One
of the next questions is which seminary you attended. Rest assured that if
was not one of the "right" ones, condescension, and even pity, will pour
forth from the vaunted alumni of the "best" schools, especially if you have
not expended the time and resources necessary to achieve a doctorate.

Is an educated clergy more important than a faithful one? That is not
a fair question, because it is not an either/or proposition. The existence of a
professional clergy class and the attitudes so many people have about it are
evidence that some place a higher value on education than on developing
and maintaining a solid prayer and devotional life. I spent seven years in
seminary in two different denominations. During that time, I learned to
read and translate Latin, Greek, and Hebrew. When I was ordained and began work as a pastor, I learned that my education meant little to the people
I served, except as it affirmed what they already believed to be true about
trained members of the clergy. Most did not want more than cursory ex-
planations from the pulpit of the meaning of the Hebrew and Greek words
behind the English words with which they were familiar, claiming that it
was boring. They wanted to know how to leverage their faith to make their
lives more prosperous and comfortable. In other words, they wanted biblical justification for their chosen lifestyles. Faith is a resource to be exploited,

not a guide for how to live. This is true of churches at every place on the theological spectrum. It is ever and always a temptation for pastors to find ways to affirm this belief, especially if it results in increased financial support and, most importantly, a higher salary.

I have enough optimism in me to hope that pastors do not mean to be condescending toward one another, but I have seen so much of it over the years. I discovered that no matter how much I accomplished or how well I did something, it was always despite my lack of training at the right institutions under the right instructors. There is a fondness among pastors for name-dropping. The only name I ever feel compelled to drop is the name of Jesus; it is the only name by which anyone can be saved. Seminary degrees will not gain us status at the judgment. Arrogance, condescension, pretentiousness, and vanity in the clergy are some of the causes of the cancer that is eating institutional Christianity alive from the inside out. There is a cure, but it is radical and most likely will not come soon enough to save the patient. Professional clergy are too invested in themselves; they will never willingly give up what they have sought so hard to attain. This is unfortunate, because the blending of religious duty and secular professionalism only adds to the perception that the church is just one more business in the world. The multimillion-dollar megachurch campuses that are sprouting up all over the country only increase the notion that pastors are just in it for the money and the prestige, especially when they devote a substantial amount of their budgets to self-promotion. Small churches do not stand a chance in that climate although some small church pastors take every possible opportunity to emulate the lifestyle of megachurch pastors and portray themselves as professionals.

Pretentiousness and vanity are not limited to clergy. Every church I have served had its share of people who wanted the ear of the head pastor. They used various means to attain this, but it often boiled down to granting financial support, especially for projects that the pastor wanted to undertake, but which were too expensive for the church budget to absorb. I desperately want to believe that financial support was offered freely, with no strings attached, but I cannot help questioning if they had the money to give, why not give it to the church for operating expenses? This question was asked when it came time to develop a church budget for the upcoming year. Every year it was simply accepted with a shrug that this was the way it was going to be, and the budget was put together accordingly. Time and again, plenty of money was available for special projects. The irony is that we rarely ended the year in the red. Somehow the money miraculously appeared. It was attributed to divine blessing, but I cannot help wondering if certain people held back so that they could jump in and rescue the church at the end of the year. I was asked more than once to forgo a raise, or to take extra vacation time in lieu of a raise, so that the budget could be met. I did not complain then because I believed that I was doing what was best for the church. I am not complaining now, only laying the groundwork for what comes next.

> The vanity of others runs counter to our taste only when it runs counter to our vanity.
>
> —FRIEDRICH NIETZSCHE, *BEYOND GOOD AND EVIL*[5]

If institutional Christianity is dying, as I am asserting, then the professional clergy class that serves it must die as well. I submit that the professional clergy are part of the reason why the church is struggling. How can a pastor be honest in his or her preaching and teaching if he or she is relying on the church for the money necessary to live? Answer: It is virtually impossible. I was once brutally honest with a church I served years ago about an issue we needed to face together, and it ultimately cost me my job as well as a piece of my soul. I chose the wrong time and method for the confrontation (Sunday morning worship) and fatally wounded any chance I may have had to remedy the situation. Given what I subsequently learned, any confrontation in any form would have been futile. They wanted compliance, not honesty. Many churches want this, which means they want membership growth without any need to change how they live, what they believe, or, especially, the way things have been done for untold generations. They want the pastor to preach uplifting sermons without making demands, bring young families into the church singlehandedly, and be a pillar in the community. I suspect that if Jesus took a job as a pastor in many small, mainline churches, he would quickly find himself unemployed.

Here is an example. Imagine a small, dying church in a small, dying community. Most of the families had been in the community for generations. The primary industry was farming, but most people worked in the surrounding towns and cities. The leadership positions in the church were passed down from generation to generation, rotating among the leading families in the church. Shortly after a young pastor arrived there and began to establish himself, the Sunday school superintendent resigned for reasons that were unclear at the time. The question was raised as to whether the pastor's wife might be interested in taking the position. The Sunday school had struggled to find teachers and perhaps "new blood" was what was needed. Against her better judgment, the pastor's wife, with her husband's urging, took the position. She began making changes that were well-received by

---

5. https://www.goodreads.com/quotes/433578-the-vanity-of-others-runs-counter-to-our-taste-only.

some but viewed with suspicion by others. The Sunday school grew and people who had been chased away by the previous leadership returned. Those who had been trying to achieve growth using the same time-honored methods repeatedly without the expected results were displeased and insulted. Passive-aggressive attacks on the pastor and his family began. After all, growth must only take place by doing what has always been done.

The only way preachers can truly proclaim the message of Jesus without compromise is if they are not relying on their "audience" for support. I am advocating, not just suggesting, that the professional clergy class cease to exist for the good of the church and the cause of Christ. Many small churches (generally defined as less than one hundred members) seek the services of non-professionals out of necessity because they do not have the resources to pay for a full-time pastor, and there are not many professionals who want to be "exiled" to a small struggling church in a small town in the middle of nowhere. Those who are willing can find themselves serving vibrant and loving churches that are only able to pay them a modest salary, at best. My experience is that small churches with part-time pastors are more likely to be engaged in collaborative ministry in their local communities than larger ones. Nonetheless, they are dismissed by large churches with full-time pastors as inferior. Yet, pastors who serve churches while holding another job to pay the bills are better able to preach, serve, and minister without compromise. The problem, many will point out, is making sure pastors have adequate training, which is expensive. The answer is twofold: Reestablish the practice of apprenticeship and simplify the amount and type of study necessary to preach, teach, administer the sacraments, and care for people pastorally. I could easily come up with a plan of study that would take no more than a year and could be done without giving up one's main vocation. While many seminaries have figured out ways to reduce or eliminate the cost of tuition, they continue to operate out of an institutional model focused on money and institution-building, not on helping people grow in their faith.

My first real experience as a pastor came the year before I was ordained. I had the privilege of serving as the student pastor of a small church in the Midwest during my final year in seminary. It was a church that had been served by student pastors for fifty years at that time. They provided a small weekly stipend and a hotel room every weekend (the church was two hours away from the seminary). Another pastor in a nearby community provided regular mentoring and guidance. The members of the church believed their God-given purpose was to help train pastors for service in the church, and they took it seriously. While they looked back fondly to the days when they were a large, flourishing church, they knew that those days were in the past and nothing was likely to change given the economics of the area. Their future was short, but they vowed to continue serving God by training pastors for as long as their money held out and for as long as there were enough people to keep it going. I served them as best I could since I was only there on the weekends. I made calls and occasionally had to make an extra trip during the week to deal with a pastoral emergency. Given the nature of the call, I also did not hold back from saying what I believed needed to be said, even when it was uninformed. I thank God frequently for their patience and understanding.

Looking back from the vantage point of time and experience, I wish that I could have kept serving that church without any need for financial compensation. It probably would not have prevented the eventual closing of the church, which happened fourteen years later, but it would have been a great lesson in what it meant to serve Jesus without catering to needs and desires that had nothing to do with the gospel. I do not have a problem with pastors being trained and educated, but I do have a problem with the notion that the clergy should be a professional class with all the attendant rights and privileges. I have spent almost three decades serving in the profession, but I do not believe Jesus intended for there to be a professional clergy. It goes against the idea that pastors are to serve, not to be served. Attempting to graft secular business models onto a spiritual endeavor effectively baptizes practices that have little to do with what Jesus intended for his followers in their efforts to carry on his mission. Case in point: Any church that has a "C-Wing" where the "executives" have their offices is an offense against everything Jesus declared about what it means to serve him as his follower. Pastors who hide behind a wall of receptionists and assistants are not following the example of Jesus. Period.

The existence of a professional clergy class creates an environment that allows people to abandon personal responsibility for faithfully living. That, after all, is what they hire the pastor to do on their behalf. It rarely ends well. Few and far between are the pastors who excel in every area of required expertise in these situations. Pastors, especially those in positions where they have no support staff, are required to be experts in all the minutia of administrative leadership while at the same time excelling in the areas of pastoral care, preaching, and teaching while maintaining regular office hours, recruiting new members, and visiting the sick and shut-ins. Often the only perceived way out of this dilemma is to add paid staff members to share the load, which exacerbates the problem. It further supports that notion that the church and its staff exist to serve the members of the church, freeing the membership from any responsibility for meaningful service. Churches without the resources to hire staff aside from the pastor expect him or her to do everything. One church I served installed a phone in the parsonage that rang whenever someone called the church, which was a few blocks away. This was built on the expectation that the pastor was always on call, even on his or her designated day off. Pastors who labor under these circumstances typically burn out within a decade and often leave the ministry or are forced to retire. Churches that have the financial wherewithal to do so expand their staff to cover responsibilities that can and should go to volunteers. This only exacerbates a consumerist attitude in and toward the church.

Another aspect of the problem is that the clergy class has been a role model for the laity from the beginning of its existence. This is both good and bad. It is good in that there have always been, by the grace of God, clergy and others who have served as exemplary models of faithfulness and service. It is just that most of them did not operate at the highest levels of church leadership. Moral depravity, open skepticism about matters of faith, and disregard for basic ethical standards may appear far less rampant now than in the past, but they are still problems in the clergy class. That is the bad part. If a pastor can twist the words of Scripture in such a way as to justify injurious behavior, he or she can lead people down the wrong path by urging them to follow his or her example. This phenomenon is glaringly evident in the ironically termed "prosperity gospel." In brief, the proponents of this gospel declare that God's greatest desire is to prosper his people. This is characterized as financial prosperity. The basic principle is this: the greater one's faith, the greater one's prosperity. Unscrupulous leaders exploit this by using it to accumulate personal wealth and expensive possessions. The point is that if God has rewarded their faith with wealth, then he certainly will not fail to fulfill theirs—so long as they continue to reward the pastor for his or her faithful preaching and service. It then becomes incumbent upon the pastor to live a lavish lifestyle as evidence of his or her faithfulness.

How ironic it is that Protestantism, which thoroughly castigated the clergy's rapacious and insatiable desire for wealth, produces churches that allow the same thing. There is a special place in hell for those who financially rape the faithful in the name of Christ. I am sure that Jesus never intended for clergy to grow rich by serving him. In fact, his words clearly indicate the opposite. The first indication that the church was straying from the original mission is recorded in the Bible, believe it or not. Shortly after they took charge, Jesus' inner circle (excluding Judas the betrayer and including his replacement Matthias) decided that it was beneath them "to serve tables" instead of devoting their time to preaching the gospel.[6] This was, arguably, a first step in the direction of a professional clergy. I submit that it was the wrong decision. Waiting on tables was exactly what Jesus

6. Acts 6:2–4.

wanted his followers to do—to *serve* one another in humility.[7] This was but the first step in elevating doctrine above action as the purest expression of faith. The earliest and, I would argue, purest expression of faith is "Jesus is Lord." Those who accept this as true acknowledge that they belong to Jesus in every meaningful sense of the word. Jesus governs what I believe and how I behave. The Gospel accounts of his life and ministry teach us all we need to know about how to live. This is a not a matter of asking "What would Jesus do?" so much as it is looking at what he did during his ministry and then doing it. Asking what Jesus would do may be trendy, but it ultimately betrays either a shallow faith or only a passing acquaintance with the Gospel accounts of Jesus' life and work. The answer is simple and obvious: Be humble, compassionate, forgiving, and selfless. None of these include demanding or requiring a reward for service—or offering payment for service.

There is a degree of irony in the story of a man named Simon (not to be confused with Simon Peter), a magician in Samaria who sought baptism in the name of Jesus after hearing the preaching of Philip, one of the earliest evangelists. Simon the magician accompanied Philip on his missionary journey and observed him performing "signs and miracles," including what became known as Holy Spirit baptism. Simon offered the apostles money in exchange for the power to do the same thing[8] and was threatened with eternal damnation as a result, but there can be little doubt that others followed his example later in the history of the institutional church. Spiritual power or benefit in exchange for money is one way of describing the doctrine of indulgences.[9] People are always looking for the easiest way to ensure eternal existence, often assuming it is possible to purchase salvation and that those who are closest to God can provide the necessary assurance that the transaction is valid. The implication is clear: professional clergy possess power and/or knowledge not accessible to the common believer. It may be that my own vanity is getting in the way here—I freely admit to the possibility. It is always easier to point out the faults of others while avoiding looking in the mirror. In my darkest moments I find myself wondering if I have accomplished anything useful for Jesus. I am neither famous nor wealthy, nor do I have a string of letters after my name. Yet, I cannot help but think based on the kind words of

7. John 13:14–16.

8. Acts 8:9–24.

9. Briefly, the idea that one can purchase credit against one's future sins or the past sins of someone who has died to decrease or eliminate the time spent in purgatory prior to entering heaven. This doctrine is based on the notion that only those who die in a state of perfect grace go immediately to heaven. Everyone else goes to purgatory where they pay for their earthly sins by enduring a specified period of suffering.

people God dropped into my life over the years that some good has come from the effort I have expended to care for folks in the name of Jesus.

> It's not vanity to know your own good points. It would just be stupidity if you didn't; it's only vanity when you get puffed up about them.
>
> —L. M. MONTGOMERY[10]

As I have noted, one central problem with the professional clergy is that its existence has a way of precluding efforts on the part of non-clergy to do what Jesus wants all his followers to do. In short, it allows anyone who has not been ordained as a pastor to take a pass on living in the way Jesus clearly intended his followers to live. Imagine what would happen if the resources devoted to supporting clergy as a professional class were instead used to help the hurting, feed the starving, and clothe the naked. Besides, many churches are not interesting in paying their pastors a wage commensurate with their education and experience. Most churches, except for the largest, wealthiest ones, avoid paying their pastor(s) more than what they believe necessary according the prevailing wages for pastors. This is one of the fundamental problems with treating churches like businesses and pastors like professions. What would happen if we all just admitted to the truth and moved to a model for ministry consistent with what Jesus intended?

Another part of the problem with a professional clergy class is that most churches, especially those that are institutional in nature, require pastors to be credentialed (i.e., to have the proper level of education). The denominational gatekeepers insist that those who want to be ordained attain a master's level degree. This means seven expensive years of college. Often this requires students to secure loans which must, of course, be repaid. Imagine leaving seminary with over $25,000 in student debt and working for a church that pays $12,000 a year, which is how I began my career in the ministry. Poverty is a reality in the professional clergy, unless you have the right connections, wealthy relatives, made a lot of money in a previous career, or have a position in a large church with abundant resources. It is no wonder that small church pastors seek ways to supplement their income. One of the churches I served paid me at a level that made me eligible for food stamps. Wanting to supplement our income, my wife got a job in a neighboring town but had to keep it secret to protect my job because the church forbade it. I suspect they thought it made them look bad.

---

10. https://www.goodreads.com/quotes/6704-it-s-not-vanity-to-know-your-own-good-points-it.

What I have learned over the years is that while there are many faithful, humble, generous Christians in the world, they are not often found in positions of power and influence in the vast national and regional bureaucracies of the institutional Church, and in some cases, even at the local level. Institutional Christianity has sold its soul to purchase the fool's gold of worldly power, wealth, and authority. That it is supposedly done in the name of spreading the gospel makes the act even more atrocious. Money and influence seem to be all that matters at many levels of the institution. Churches that have neither are forced out to the margins from which vantage point they look upon the proclamations of the leadership with cynicism and skepticism. People are abandoning churches of every theological persuasion, size, and composition because they do not believe they can make a meaningful contribution unless they are willing to believe what they are told and give what they are told while those in power dictate the direction of the church, the programs to be undertaken, and the way the church will function.

Vanity and hypocrisy are rife in the church because many people are unwilling to admit the truth or, if they recognize it, unwilling to fight for it. We love lies and hate the truth because lies are comfortable, and the truth is painful. Lies encourage us to seek comfort while the truth challenges us. When confronted with the truth, our first impulse is to kill, or at least mortally wound, the messenger. This is at least part of the reason why so many pastors who entered the ministry with a deep sense of God's call are doing something else and why so many of us leave the ministry within five years of entering it. People would rather be comfortable than admit the truth. Although I describe myself as an optimist, I am reluctantly realistic about the demise of institutional Christianity in the Western world as we know it today. We claim to want the truth, but the truth is that we would rather embrace lies. The truth sets us free, but bondage to lies often seems more comfortable. Pockets of faithfulness persist in nearly every expression of institutional Christianity; good things are indeed happening, which gives me some hope. But there is no reason for lasting hope so long as institutional Christianity clings stubbornly to the lies that give it a false sense of comfort and security.

Chapter 10

Truth Sets You Free,
Unless You Like Bondage

If you tell the truth, you don't have to remember anything.

—Mark Twain[1]

"What is truth?" Pontius Pilate cynically asked Jesus at his trial.[2] Francis Bacon, essayist, philosopher, and contemporary of Shakespeare, began his essay "Of Truth" with this question and opined that people know the difference between truth and lies but disdain the truth because our natural inclination is to love lies, in part because uncovering the truth can be difficult and time-consuming, if not downright uncomfortable. Our reluctance to embrace the truth instead of lies rests on other factors as well. The truth is hard and unyielding while lies are often soft and comfortable. The truth forces us to face reality in all its harshness while lies allow us to hide from personal responsibility and accountability. This may be one reason why so many in our modern world are hopelessly confused about how to differentiate between truth and falsehood. Institutional Christianities frequently aggravate this by blurring or finessing the truth in the interests of tolerance and acceptance. Popular notions to the contrary, it is possible to discover and learn the truth, if by no other means than by definitively identifying what is false.

This is all counter-cultural in an era when truth, if it is acknowledged to exist at all, is declared to be fluid, shifting, relative, and personal. While I vigorously defend the notion that people are free to believe as they wish, belief does not determine reality. This should be glaringly self-evident,

1. https://www.brainyquote.com/quotes/mark_twain_133066.

2. "Pilate asked him, 'What is truth?' After he had said this, he went out to the Jews again and told them, 'I find no case against him'" (John 18:38).

but reality does not seem to play a role in determining the truth, at least in the realms of ethics and morality. It is asserted, apparently without the slightest bit of irony, that everyone is entitled to his or her truth even if it is the opposite of what someone else claims to be true. In short, there are no absolute truths except the absolute truth that there is no absolute truth. George Orwell, wherever he may be now apart from the grave in which his corporeal form is moldering, must be feeling very proud. The purveyors of this pseudo-philosophical garbage need to know that their vaunted ideas are not new. Philosophers have played hard and fast with the truth for as long as the concept of truth has been around. Despite all claims to the contrary, truth is not relative, but it can be uncomfortable when it challenges our comfort and sense of security. The irony is that the institutional church claims to be the purveyor of truth while simultaneously declaring that there is no absolute truth. This may best be characterized as "whatever I want to believe–ism" and is most clearly demonstrated in Western Christianity by Unitarian Universalism. The relativization of truth leads inexorably to the relativization of ethics and morality, which in turn has a deleterious effect on all aspects of human society and culture.

There are two sides to every question.

—PROTAGORAS[3]

Moral (or ethical) relativism is not a new phenomenon. It goes back to the time of Protagoras (490–420 BC), the first person believed to have made a living as a college professor (not what they would have called it then), paving the way for a professorial class. Traveling frauds and charlatans soon abounded since even the appearance of being highly educated was enough to fool naïve people into parting with their hard-earned cash in exchange for special knowledge of dubious provenance. Itinerant teachers and preachers travelled from city to city hoping to find receptive audiences for the pseudo-intellectual gems they were selling and make a little money in the process. This inevitably led to the practice of tailoring one's teaching to the preferences of one's benefactors. When you are doing it for money there is always the temptation to tell those who are paying you what you believe they want to hear. This applies to nearly every profession, from the oldest to the newest, if you catch my drift. It was and is true of institutional Christianity, and while it is tempting to name names, it is enough to say that preachers who promise health, wealth, and prosperity without any meaningful commitment to Jesus are following in the footsteps of these shameless ancient purveyors of spiritual and philosophical pornography. The lure

3. https://www.brainyquote.com/quotes/protagoras_205541.

of moral relativism and pornography are the same: the hollow promise of pleasure without effort or commitment. It is an appealing lie that slithers out of the pits of hell.

Moral relativism and intentional manipulation of the truth have festered in institutional Christianity since at least the fourth century AD. We have already seen how an eighth-century forgery, the *Donation of Constantine*, was cynically used by people who should have known better to promote the belief that the pope of the Roman Catholic Church was not only the spiritual lord of Christendom but was also the supreme ruler of a swath of prime territory in central Italy. It did not end there. Once accepted as fact by the rulers of Europe, the principles set forth in the *Donation* were utilized by successive popes to claim for themselves the sole power to make and unmake every king, emperor, and ruler on the planet. No one could be a legitimate ruler without the pope's blessing. This led to embarrassing scenes in which rulers of far greater moral integrity and political power than the man occupying the Chair of Peter abased themselves before him, kissed his feet, and cravenly sought his blessing, which he bestowed in exchange for personal benefit, all the while claiming that it was all for the good of the church and the world.

Is it any wonder that unscrupulous men were willing to commit murder and other atrocities to attain and maintain such a prize? Many of the popes in that benighted age blithely ignored the truth when it served their interests and cynically perverted it when it was to their benefit. Giovanni de Medici, who ruled the Roman Catholic Church as Leo X from 1513 to 1521, is reported to have written to his brother, "God has given us the papacy, let us enjoy it!" upon his election, seeing it not as a responsibility but as a tasty dish to relish.[4] Leo commissioned Raphael to immortalize the *Donation of Constantine* (by then discredited) in an enormous fresco. He chose to embrace the lie because it had helped create, support, and strengthen the temporal power of the papacy. Leo was, it must be said, a man of his times and for him to acknowledge the truth would have meant relinquishing a lucrative position of power—one that would enable him to elevate his family and establish them as landholding members of the aristocracy. Relinquishing temporal authority would also have plunged Europe even further into chaos as various powers fought to gain control over the territories held by the papacy.

In my experience, some people will embrace whatever version of the truth best helps them gain control and exercise power over others. They do not always do it knowingly or willingly, but do so, nonetheless. And they will engage in Olympic–level moral and intellectual gymnastics to justify

4. Chamberlin, *Bad Popes*, 210.

their actions and motivations. Sometimes it can be attributed to cowardice, sometimes to self-preservation, and sometimes to deliberate, cynical
manipulation of the truth for a "greater purpose." Many a monstrous atrocity has been committed by those who knew better but were "just following orders" to save their own skin. How many former Nazi officers used
that defense? Is it self-deception, cowardice, self-preservation, or malice?
I would argue that in the case of institutional Christianity it is both all and
none of the above.

Cowardice pervades our culture. No one seems willing to stand up
to the purveyors of blatant falsehoods stridently proclaiming the sanctity
of their causes and loudly decrying anyone who dares to contradict them.
This is especially true when it comes to the relationship between organized
religion and money. Religious institutions need money to operate, but how
much is enough? Churches that dedicate 10, 20, and even 50 percent of
their budget to mission work and charity experience a degree of pride and
satisfaction, but unless they are devoting more to mission than to maintaining their facility, then they are not really doing what Jesus wants them to
do. Resources utilized for building upkeep and maintenance, salaries, and
furnishings cannot be used to help the hurting. Churches make all kinds of
excuses for this disparity, including the assertion that a well-appointed facility is necessary to adequately train people for service in the field. Yet, if the
statistics are true, only about 20 percent of the members in any given church
are involved in any sort of outreach or ministry. This happens for a variety
of reasons, but I suspect it often involves some degree of self-deception. The
truth is that, referencing the old tale, the emperor is naked, and the assertion that his fine new clothes are visible only to those who are worthy is a lie
fabricated by bold, creative thieves. Cowardice can lead to suppression or
denial of truth. It seems that much sadder today considering current battles
over the validity of the Bible.

> Properly read, the Bible is the most potent force for atheism ever
> conceived.
>
> —Isaac Asimov[5]

It is fair to say that Bible has undergone intense scrutiny and attack
since at least the time of the Enlightenment. It has been used both to prove
and disprove the existence of God. This is an observation, not a complaint.
I have witnessed firsthand how sincere attempts to analyze and interpret
the Bible have been perceived as attacks on its validity. I first started reading the Bible in earnest when I began attending Roman Catholic seminary

5. https://www.azquotes.com/quote/367622.

two years after I graduated from high school. I remember an Old Testament class my first year that focused mainly on understanding the methods of interpretation developed in Germany during the late nineteenth and early twentieth century. My seminary classmates and I began our journey through the Old Testament by learning how scholars had assigned different verses, parts of verses, and even individual words to one of four schools of authors, none of whom could be definitively identified. It was staggering to contemplate. Remember: I grew up at a time when Catholics were not generally encouraged to read or study the Bible independently. Some of my classmates openly rebelled against anything that called into question traditional beliefs concerning human authorship and divine inspiration. I vividly remember one classmate violently (and somewhat rudely) confronting the priest teaching the class, stopping just short of accusing him of heresy.[6] It did not seem like a big deal to me at the time because I did not know much about the Bible, but it planted a seed in my consciousness, one that grew over the years into a tree of doubt.

Have you ever had your most basic beliefs called into question? My first experience in seminary fundamentally challenged what I had always believed to be true. Many of the priests who publicly taught the traditions privately (and sometimes not so privately) called into question long-held doctrines and beliefs. Then there was the culture of preference and favoritism that focused on students from well-connected families or who openly flaunted tradition. Seminarians who displayed conservative beliefs and tendencies were called on the carpet and reprimanded, while those who flagrantly and flamboyantly flaunted the rules were praised and celebrated. You do not have to take my word for it: an excellent book describes this in detail.[7] I believe that some of the priests who taught us did not believe what they were teaching but kept silent having been pressured to conform by those who sought the destruction of the church. My understanding of celibacy, clerical authority, moral integrity, the value of ritual, and the reliability of the Bible were called into question during the four years that I spent discerning a vocation to the priesthood. I am pleased to report that attitudes and practices have changed in the diocese in which I did my training, but it came far too late for me, most of my classmates, and some of the priests under whom I studied.

The pressure to compromise one's deeply held principles and keep quiet to keep one's job is, I believe, at least part of what produced the unhappiness

6. I learned recently that this individual has disavowed religion completely and claims to be an atheist.

7. Rose, *Goodbye, Good Men.* I attended one of the seminaries mentioned in this book.

I sensed in the priests under whose care we were placed. They were being pressured to teach a new version of the truth, one that did not correspond to what they had learned during their own training. This new truth was supposed to set them free from the tyranny of the past, but mostly what it did was chain them to an impossible reality characterized by emotional, spiritual, ethical, and moral dissonance. It is no wonder that some of them sought comfort in alcohol, drugs, and illicit sexual activities with boys, girls, men, and women. Lies may bring us immediate comfort, but they ultimately produce only misery and death. The lies we tell others are dangerous for many reasons, but the lies we tell ourselves are deadly. One of the priests with whom I studied committed suicide after years of desperately trying to heal his pain with alcohol. Another was stripped of his credentials and his ordination in the wake of accusations of sexual misconduct. His best friend left the priesthood to marry a woman he had been seeing while he was still a priest. Most of the rest found their way back into parish ministry where they hopefully found some measure of contentment and peace.

The truth is rarely pure and never simple.

—Oscar Wilde[8]

What is truth? Does knowing the truth matter anymore? Truth has become so relative in these increasingly dystopian times that we reflexively label as "fake news" anything with which we disagree regardless of any truth it might contain. The truth is rapidly becoming a subjective weapon in the war to impose one set of values upon the culture to the exclusion of all others in the name of tolerance. This happens at every point on the ideological spectrum. The line between reporting the news and commenting on the news has been blurred to such a degree that it is difficult to discern what is objective news and what is subjective opinion. We are more interested in promoting *our* truth than we are in uncovering *the* truth. If you identify as a conservative, your truth is automatically dismissed by progressives. The opposite is obviously the case as well. This is also true in the religious realm, but I would argue that the consequences there are much more worrisome. In usurping for ourselves the right to decide what is true and what it false, we have taken upon ourselves the authority to define what constitutes the parameters of correct belief and practice. This has eternal consequences.

It fascinates me that the religious movements spawned by the Protestant Reformation (many of which became institutions) returned to what they rejected in breaking free from Roman Catholicism.[9] Chief among this

8. https://www.brainyquote.com/quotes/oscar_wilde_101825.

9. It has happened to them according to the true proverb, "The dog turns back to its

corruption is that the rejection of the pope's claim to be the sole arbiter of the truth in all matters of scriptural interpretation was quickly followed by efforts on the part of Protestant leaders and scholars to make the same claim. My first seminary experience revealed that many practicing Catholics are not willing to cede ultimate authority to the pope. One problem is that their ability to properly interpret Scripture is largely uninformed. It should surprise no one to learn that many Catholics are publicly faithful but privately reject Church teachings on birth control, homosexuality, and divorce. They justify their rejection by pointing out the obviously hypocrisy of being told by pedophiles and adulterers that using birth control is sinful. Members of the Roman Catholic Church are required to adhere to doctrine, but enforcement is rare unless the violator is a prominent politician. Roman Catholicism is losing any remaining authority it had to pronounce moral judgment on its members. Many are leaving the Roman Catholic Church to seek one that better reflects what they believe, but they may not like what they find. Vocal constituencies in every Christian denomination are working to undermine essential doctrines in the name of progress, an effort that is creating the kind of ethically and morally permissive environment that led to the current problems among the Catholic clergy. The truth is never simple, which may be why it is so hard for some people to grasp and accept. The prostitution of truth to the false god of hedonistic relativism in the effort to make it simple to understand has hastened the demise of institutional Christianity.

Let us not give Protestantism a pass. I thought I had left skepticism about the Bible aside when I left Roman Catholicism. It seemed to me, at least for a while, that Protestants had a deeper respect for Scripture. I soon learned that I was mistaken. I was told by educated professionals that enlightened Christians understood that the Bible is not to be trusted because it was written by men who lived in a patriarchal culture. Even more damning is the assertion that since the Bible was written by the victors of theological, religious, and doctrinal wars, it is untrustworthy. The greatest irony is the claim by certain scholars that they could determine which of Jesus' words recorded in the Bible he really spoke, which may have a kernel of historical truth, which are myth, and which pronouncements must be dismissed as mere statements of the early church and are therefore not authoritative. It cannot possibly be a coincidence that the rejected statements are those that run counter to modern ethical and moral assertions. This has less to do with the Bible than it does with who claims the authority to interpret the Bible for those judged to be too ignorant to understand it. The malicious

---

own vomit," and "The sow is washed only to wallow in the mud" (2 Pet 2:22).

lie is that only those with the proper education and, more importantly, the correct moral perspective can interpret the Bible accurately. There are countless problems with this approach. Interpreting the Bible is a matter of which "lens" you look through as you read it. The best, and arguably the most accurate, lens is the one through which the earliest readers/hearers looked. Utilizing this lens requires a level of effort that many seem unwilling to bring to the endeavor. It requires understanding that while truth is not relative, there are different kinds of truth.

Please understand this: I am neither fundamentalist nor liberal in my efforts to read and interpret the Bible. For example, I do not believe that the story of creation as recorded in the first two chapters of Genesis is literally true from a scientific perspective. Nor do I reject it as allegory. Instead, the creation story must be understood first and foremost as a story that truly tells us about God and his relation to creation. It must be read with an awareness of the cosmology that prevailed when it was written down (probably the seventh century BC).[10] The focus is not on the mechanics of the creation process, but on the purpose for which God created. There is no "how," only "why" and "for what purpose." To that end, the aim of the creation account is to assert that God designed the world and brought it into being to provide a place in which the pinnacle of his creation, humanity, could live and thrive. We run into countless problems when we insist that the Bible encompass every possible truth in every aspect of human life. The Bible is a book about spiritual, moral, and ethical truths. It was never intended to be a science textbook.

This is important for several reasons. The first one matters only if you expect and/or believe that human life continues in some form after death. If this is not your thing, then feel free to skip ahead. All set? Here we go: It is not within our power to decide what reality looks like and how it behaves. As far as I know, no one has yet figured out how to change the rotation of the earth, move the planet from its orbit, or cause the sun to rise in the west. If there is a "place" to which the soul, spirit, essence, or consciousness goes after we die, then it stands to reason that human beings had nothing to do with creating it. If we did not participate in its creation, then we have no right to decide who and how one gets there. This does not stop us from trying. It never ceases to amaze me how Christians of every ideological persuasion unabashedly convince themselves, and try to convince others, that they alone possess the "keys" to heaven and hell. This is nonsense. Equally absurd is the claim that all religions offer an equally valid path to heaven.

10. You will benefit immensely from reading *The Lost World of Genesis One* by John Walton.

There is a truth to be discovered here, one rooted in the uniqueness of Jesus and an oft-misunderstood declaration he made about how to get to heaven. You have probably heard it, but let me quote it here in its entirety:

> "Let not your hearts be troubled. Believe in God; believe also in me. In my Father's house are many rooms. If it were not so, would I have told you that I go to prepare a place for you? And if I go and prepare a place for you, I will come again and will take you to myself, that where I am you may be also. And you know the way to where I am going." Thomas said to him, "Lord, we do not know where you are going. How can we know the way?" Jesus said to him, "*I am the way*, and the truth, and the life. No one comes to the Father *except through me.*[11]

Pay close attention to the question and answer. Thomas asked, "How can we *know* the way?" Jesus responded by declaring, "*I* am the way." Thomas asked for knowledge and a method; Jesus pointed him toward a person. The point: You get to heaven by following a person, not a program. And not just *any* person. Why? Simple: Any program with that kind of power placed in human hands can and will be perverted for nefarious purposes. It will be used to oppress, rob, destroy, humiliate, and imprison people, as history as shown. Please do not lose sight of the fact that when Jesus said these words there was no such thing as Christianity or the church, nor did he mention it anywhere in the discourse containing these words. Let me be clear: The institutional Church does not have the power to save anyone. Neither does any program, mode of behavior, list of requirements, or doctrinal assertions promoted by any religion anywhere in the world. That is the truth, and it will set you free in so many ways.

The notion that every religion contains some truth is noble but naïve. This sentiment is most often expressed, in my opinion, by those who are afraid of offending others. Been there, done that, but no more. Life is too short. There are plenty of religions in the world that are based on outright lies, yet people are taken in by their claims.[12] Charismatic leaders form cults that delude people into giving up their possessions, their morality, their freedom, and even their lives simply because someone claims a "special revelation" (Oh, how I hate that phrase!) from God. It is sad that Christians are so willing to be shamed into silence because of the crimes committed by the church in the name of Jesus centuries ago. I will not accept personal blame or shame for these crimes. Jesus does not approve of them. Why he allowed them in the first place is a question for which I do not have a ready answer.

---

11. John 14:1–6, ESV, emphasis added.

12. Jim Jones and David Koresh are two obvious examples.

He did warn us, however, to "Beware of false prophets, who come to you in sheep's clothing but inwardly are ravenous wolves."[13] It is to the church's lasting shame that many false prophets robed themselves in splendor and claimed to be the temporal and spiritual successors of Peter, robbing and murdering in the name of serving Jesus. They were indeed ravenous wolves. The poison they spewed out in the name of Jesus continues to spread today, infecting every expression of Christianity.

Denominationalism is an aberration and so is institutional Christianity. The church is at its best when it is small and focused on serving, not on being served.[14] The life Jesus wants us to live in service to him is foreign to the values of the Western world. We westerners only want to serve when it is convenient, fits our busy schedules, and is not so costly that is detracts from our desired level of comfort. This is one of the diseases that infects institutional Christianity. Institutional Christianity goes to great lengths to characterize low-commitment, convenient, low-impact service as Christian service. It allows churches to characterize social justice posturing (carrying a placard and protesting) as mission work. The hope is that such behavior will attract new members, but the truth is that the few new members they might draw in, while initially enthusiastic, soon drift away for lack of interest in an institution that is largely focused on navel-gazing, building more buildings to make room for more butts in the pews and hopefully put more bucks in the offering plate.

> The truth will set you free, but first it will piss you off.
>
> —Joe Klaas[15]

The truth can be difficult, painful, and more than a little challenging; it can, indeed, piss you off if you disagree with it. This may be a few of the reasons why we cling so desperately to lies while deliberately rejecting the truth. The easy path often appears far more beneficial than it is. In truth, the impulse to cling to lies and reject the truth is as much a function of cowardice as anything else. (I speak from personal experience.) The desire to avoid conflict, overwhelming for some of us, leads us to embrace ideas and assertions that are in complete opposition to our deeply held values, simply because we do not want to make waves or challenge the status quo. I am as guilty of this as anyone. I have looked the other way when church

13. "Watch out for false prophets. They come to you in sheep's clothing, but inwardly they are ferocious wolves" (Matt 7:15, NIV).

14. This is one principle behind the development of small groups, the focus of much of my ministry.

15. https://www.goodreads.com/quotes/11090-the-truth-will-set-you-free-but-first-it-will.

members engaged in behavior that was clearly sinful because I was afraid of the consequences of confronting them. A fair number of couples who sought me out to perform their weddings did so after they had been told by their own pastor that he would not marry them because they were already living together. Weddings were a lucrative source of extra income for me, and the material we used for marriage preparation included a section for cohabiting couples. Even though my every spiritual instinct told me this was wrong, I agreed to do the weddings, provided the couples went through the required counseling. It should come as no surprise that many of those marriages ended in divorce, some of them quickly.[16]

I find it more than a little interesting that some of the churches, sects, and movements that *are* experiencing growth these days are the ones that have the most stringent requirements for their members. This has been true throughout the history of religion in general and particularly in Christianity. Mormons, Jehovah's Witness, and Islam all see modest increases in their overall membership whenever mainline churches experience decline. Perhaps the one exception to this is the Roman Catholic Church, but membership gains in some parts of the world are offset by losses in others, especially in the global West. Catholics are abandoning the church in droves in response to the latest scandals and the pope's apparent unwillingness to act decisively in response to credible accusations of abuse. The adoption of liberal ethical and moral standards has done more harm than good to the cause of institutional Christianity. Nonetheless, some mainline denominations have adopted the strategy of ascribing to more liberal standards to attract new members, but doing so has not significantly helped. When the church becomes indistinguishable from a social club it loses some of its luster, especially if it requires its members to donate money to dubious causes and to give up precious family time on Sunday.

I know what it means to be part of a church that places obligations on its members. I grew up in a traditional Roman Catholic household. It was traditional is the sense that we faithfully obeyed the requirement to attend Mass every weekend and on every holy day, even though religious practices were not part of our daily experience at home. There were no religious icons on the wall, no family devotions, and no daily recitation of the rosary.[17] I did not even know what a rosary was until I was twelve and spent a few days one summer with my hyper-Catholic aunts. I was made to understand that weekly mass attendance was a requirement and there were spiritual

16. One couple who had been living together for nine years prior to their marriage divorced less than a year later.

17. This is an observation, not a criticism, and was the reality for other Catholic families I knew growing up.

consequences for disregarding it. Despite my fear of eternal damnation (to the degree that I understood it), I found myself drawn to the rituals of the church. When asked to serve our parish as an altar boy, I readily accepted, believing that it would bring me closer to God. To make a long story short, my involvement in this capacity so softened my heart that when I felt the call to enter the ministry, I did not question it and responded immediately.

There is truth, and then there is Truth. The former is fluid, the latter dismissed as the rigid panacea of the unenlightened. How ironic it is that we, the philosophical descendants of Plato and Aristotle, reject the notion that there can be absolute truth! We would prefer, apparently, to bind ourselves with chains of our own forging to debilitating lies. This is destroying the institutional Church. The lies institutional Christianities enthusiastically embrace in the name of tolerance, acceptance, and love do not further the cause of Christ. In fact, they do great harm because they promote a level of moral ambiguity not seen since the most decadent days of the papacy in the Middle Ages. Why are we so afraid to stand up for the truth? I suspect the motives are mixed, at best. In some cases, it is cowardice. In others it is a cynical attempt to control the hearts and minds of people to gain power and control over them. Significant parts of institutional Christianity are guilty of this and will ultimately pay the price. The truth sets us free, but it is rarely the easy, comfortable truth the world promotes. Instead, it is the truth that pisses us off, requiring dedication, sacrifice and the willingness to stand fast in the face of every attack against us. Christianity knew how to do this early in its history in the towns and villages of Judea and Samaria, but its successors in the West have forgotten and will perish as a result.

Chapter 11

Is it Cowardice or Self-Preservation?

> In a word, I was too cowardly to do what I knew to be right, as I
> had been too cowardly to avoid doing what I knew to be wrong.
>
> —Charles Dickens[1]

It occurred to me as I was thinking about the previous chapter that the problems our culture has with truth might not be due to deliberate manipulation of the truth. Instead, it may have more to do with ignorance, cowardice, or peer pressure. This makes sense if we look at it from the perspective of warfare. I recently read a fascinating memoir written by a German soldier who served on the Russian Front in the Second World War. Willy Reese was, by his own admission, deeply opposed to the war and the fascist mindset that produced and pursued it at the cost of millions of lives. Yet, he responded promptly and willingly when drafted, participated in his training, and obediently followed orders when his unit was sent to Russia. Willy honestly recounts how he and his comrades pillaged and plundered as they made their way across the frozen Russian countryside. But he also describes the emotional dissonance and separation that enabled him to callously deprive others of what they needed to live so that he could survive. At some level Willy recognized that what he was doing was wrong, but he did what he had to do to make it to the next minute, hour, and day. His post-war stories would have been fascinating but he did not live to see the end of the war, dying in battle at the end of June 1944.[2]

This is a well-documented phenomenon and a crucial element in the "just following orders" defense adopted by some of those accused of wartime atrocities. We may shake our head, wag our finger, and declare that

1. https://www.azquotes.com/quote/344316.
2. Reese, *Stranger to Myself.*

there is no excuse for such behavior, but the reality is that we do the same thing, maybe not always or often to the same degree, and engage in all kinds of philosophical gymnastics to justify it. Justification is only helpful for the winners. As has been opined numerous times, the winners write the history and the losers are tried for war crimes. There is a certain subjectivity inherent in the evaluation of wartime actions. One side's justifiable action is the other side's atrocity. Which is the greater atrocity: the deaths of six million Jews at the hands of the Nazis in death camps, the deaths of a quarter to a half million people who perished immediately and over a period of decades as a direct result of the atomic bombs the United States dropped on Hiroshima and Nagasaki, or the untold millions who died or disappeared during Stalin's brutal regime? Critics complain that history is unreliable precisely because it was written by the victors, and to some extent that is true. The bigger issue is not so much how the victors write their own stories as it is the irresistible temptation to rewrite history well after the fact for purposes of propaganda and reeducation. Lenin, Stalin, and their successors perfected this, but they were only following a custom already well established in Asia and Europe. Catherine the Great (1729–1796), who was born in Poland and of German ancestry, married into the ruling Russian Romanov family and deposed her deeply unpopular half-Russian husband in a coup. Painfully aware of her non-Russian pedigree, she spared no effort in diminishing her ethnic pedigree while working to emphasize her unimpeachable ideological connection to the thoroughly Russian Peter the Great (1672–1725). About a century later, on being elected emperor of France in 1804, an ambitious Corsican soldier with grand plans for himself named Napoleon (1769–1821) deliberately chose the bee as his personal and family emblem because it was associated with the Merovingian dynasty of Childeric I (437–481), the thoroughly French king who made France a sovereign nation.

There is a fine line between self-preservation and cowardice. History is written by the victors as a way of solidifying a genetic or ideological pedigree. History is also sometimes written or rewritten by those who are seeking the patronage or support of the victors. This can be a form of cowardice when the writer deliberately hides the truth because it is unflattering or otherwise damaging. None of this means that the accounts are false or completely unreliable, only that they are biased toward a specific point of view. Tragically, the rewriting of history, under the guise of "new research," is one of the reasons why institutional Christianity is fading rapidly into obscurity, at least in the Western world.

One aspect of this is the effort to distinguish between what words Jesus spoke and what words the Gospel writers put on his lips. It is noble but misguided because it puts all of what he said under a cloud of doubt and suspicion.

This is not a new phenomenon, having its roots in the so-called "Quest for the Historical Jesus" that arose in Europe in the eighteenth century, most notably in Germany. These quests, although popular among the intelligentsia, failed in their efforts because they did not account for Jesus' identity as a faithful Jew of his time. Some scholars sought to completely divorce him from his Jewishness. Others reimagined Jesus to make him fit whatever bias they wanted to use him to promote, separating him from his historical context in the process. This was due in part to the scarcity of historical data available at the time. A general prejudice against all things Jewish must also be acknowledged, especially given what happened under the Nazi regime in the early twentieth century. Political considerations aside, the problem with these quests is that they begin with the image of Jesus that they believe to be true and then sift through the Gospels for evidence that supports it, dismissing every element that does not conform to their theory as a creation of the early church.

This is still glaringly obvious today. Institutional Christianities, whether they be liberal, progressive, conservative, or evangelical, deliberately set out to interpret the Bible in the way that best supports their continued existence. The most obvious example is the Roman Catholic Church, which continues to insist that the pope is the direct spiritual descendant of Peter, based on their interpretation of a single verse in the Gospel of Matthew. This is problematic for any number of reasons, but one that stands out is the vast wealth the church holds in the form of land, buildings, artwork, and liquid assets. The preponderance of possessions is difficult to justify given Jesus' great concern for the poor. Paraphrasing Martin Luther (the sixteenth century reformer not the twentieth century activist): If the pope really believes he is the successor of Peter and that he is responsible for carrying on the mission of Jesus, then why does he not sell the vast possessions of the church and use it to help people? Answer: The institution is more important than the people it claims to serve. The best course of action is to liquidate the assets of the church and use the proceeds to help the needy. Unfortunately, the vast bureaucracy that is the church lacks the courage to do the right thing, choosing instead to promote its own self-preservation. I wonder if the most recent abuse scandals will change anything.

Let us not give Protestantism a pass. Look at the huge well-appointed buildings that serve as denominational headquarters and the generous salary packages lavished upon those who spend their time administering the institution instead of caring for people. See how they hold conferences in resorts and luxury hotels where the latest technologies are ostentatiously on display and attendees are encouraged to spend thousands of dollars on the best and most current resources available. Watch and listen as these supposedly humble servants of Jesus complain about slow internet access, brag about how often they need to check in with their assistants, and bemoan having to wait in line for their five dollar diet mocha latte while treating the people serving them as their obvious inferiors. Question: How do they justify their behavior in view of their alleged identity as faithful servants of Jesus? Answer: They do not, considering it their just due as the educated professionals they believe themselves to be. Apparently, they have chosen to ignore what Jesus said about how his followers should act in the world: "If anyone would come after me, let him deny himself and take up his cross daily and follow me."[3] The only cross many of these people know is the cross of a non-gourmet cup of coffee and an insufficient number of outlets where they can charge their (appropriately) power-hungry iPhones and iPads. Their justification for this may be found in the apostle Paul's admonition that "the ox not be muzzled when it treads out the grain,"[4] but the reality is that many pastors aspire to a lifestyle that Jesus rejected out of hand for those who believe they are called to serve him. Pastors who openly present themselves as wealthy and technologically sophisticated may impress one another, but they critically wound their ability to witness to the poor, outcast, and disenfranchised, the very people they seem so concerned to help. Talk is cheap; actions are what ultimately matter.

> On some positions, cowardice asks the question, is it expedient? And then expedience comes along and asks the question, is it politic? Vanity asks the question, is it popular? Conscience asks the question, is it right?
>
> —MARTIN LUTHER KING JR.[5]

Churches that function like institutions and pastors who behave like secular professionals can never hope to effectively accomplish Jesus' counter-cultural mission with any degree of lasting success. Some will undoubtedly object that Jesus told his followers to be *in* the world but not *of* the world. This is an unfortunate, hopefully unintentional, amalgamation of several Bible passages, the core verses being John 17:14–16.[6] It is undeniable that we are in the world so long as we are alive. The point is that we are not

---

3. "Then he said to them all, 'If any want to become my followers, let them deny themselves and take up their cross daily and follow me'" (Luke 9:23).

4. "For it is written in the Law of Moses, 'You shall not muzzle an ox when it treads out the grain.' Is it for oxen that God is concerned?" (1 Cor 9:9, ESV).

5. https://www.azquotes.com/quote/348300.

6. "I have given them your word, and the world has hated them because they are not of the world, just as I am not of the world. I do not ask that you take them out of the world, but that you keep them from the evil one. They are not of the world, just as I am not of the world" (John 17:14–16, ESV).

supposed to conform to the ways of the world, a statement with which the apostle Paul was in full agreement.[7] Church buildings that resemble college campuses, worship spaces that look like auditoriums, and pastors who function like corporate CEOs are fully in *and* of the world. Experts on church growth (who sometimes have little or no experience serving a local church) have convinced institutional Christianity that the best way to attract young people (touted as the future of the church) is by being trendy, not being too traditional (whatever that means) and avoiding anything ritualistic or "churchy." I feel confident that history will prove this to be a falsehood equal in devastation to the lie a serpent told a man and woman in a garden long ago. Institutional Christianity has sold its soul to worldly wealth and power at the cost of its life. The tragedy is not the demise of the institution but the fact that so many Christians have bought into the fiction that while religion may provide *suggestions* as to what we should believe, the world best determines how we live. Here is the lie: The serpent told Adam and Eve that despite what they had been told they would not die if they ate the forbidden fruit.[8] The serpent failed to tell them that immediately upon eating the forbidden fruit they would lose their God-given immortality and that their sin would have cosmic ramifications for the entire human race. Look around: Adam and Eve are dead. The church will die. Jesus' mission, and those who are faithful to him, will live.

Jesus does not need institutional Christianity to accomplish his mission, which is a good thing! Christians are a minority in the places where the movement was born. Palestine and Asia Minor still harbor small communities that face increasing persecution from majority Muslim populations. Yet they continue to attract new believers even as they face an uncertain future. Institutional Christianity in the West does not seem to care about the fate of Christians in these places, apparently accepting that Islam should be dominant in the East—something that has been true since for the past five centuries. They naively believe that the future of Christianity is firmly rooted in the West even as they look to Jerusalem as the place where Jesus will return, asserting that it is his job to straighten out what is happening there. This is not to say that it is our duty to urge military intervention. Rather, we must seriously consider what we are called to do spiritually for the persecuted Christians in the region beyond simply praying for their welfare and denouncing Israel as an unjust occupier of the region. Institutional Christianities in the developed world are dying while Pentecostal Christianities are

---

7. "Do not be conformed to this world, but be transformed by the renewal of your mind, that by testing you may discern what is the will of God, what is good and acceptable and perfect" (Rom 12:2, ESV).

8. "But the serpent said to the woman, 'You will not die'" (Gen 3:4).

flourishing in Africa, to the dismay of institutional Christians throughout the West. Churches in Africa assent to moral and ethical value systems that western progressives have dismissed as antiquated and intolerant. The former grow while the latter struggle to survive. One reason is that African churches present Christianity as a visceral experience of a deep, meaningful relationship with Jesus. Institutional Christians of the progressive persuasion claim to care about social justice, but it is telling that their efforts fail to address the deepest problems in our society: homelessness, poverty, drug abuse, and the like. Instead they focus on the trendy issues that affect far fewer people than the real, pervasive, and endemic issues mentioned above. Institutional Christianity will not survive by conforming to the world. It may achieve a temporary reprieve from death, but it is clear from the words of Jesus that the church and the world stand in opposition to one another.

> The opposite of courage in our society is not cowardice, it's conformity.
>
> —ROLLO MAY[9]

Conformity is a positive value in some segments of society. It is not always or often true conformity; instead, it is acquiescence to values that challenge the least number of people. Institutional Christians conform to the world in ways that are not appropriate for followers of Jesus. Their actions are culturally acceptable even if they clearly violate the clear word of Scripture. Abortion and adultery are two obvious examples, but there are more. Christians gossip, lie, lust, covet, drink to excess, take God's name in vain, and think murderous thoughts without any sense of guilt. The faithful notice, as does the world. Sometimes we acquiesce or keep silent because we do not want to be perceived as snobs or self-righteous in the eyes of friends and colleagues. How many times have you gone along with a cruel joke or laughed at a sarcastic quip made at someone's expense even if you were cringing inside? We decry the misuse of peer pressure when it involves young people, but blithely submit to it as adults, fearing rejection like a timid teenager trying to secure a date for the prom. This has always been true but seems to be more prevalent and insidious now. We are at war on multiple fronts. I am not talking about conflicts with other countries, which always take place and are easily identified. The war I am talking about is being waged using weapons that are insidiously, perhaps intentionally, designed to destroy the fabric of society. It is taking place in the halls of government, the classrooms of schools at every level, in churches of all sizes, and across the internet.

9. https://www.azquotes.com/quote/190640.

What is this war and why does it matter? It is no less than a battle for the heart and soul of our culture. There are forces within our culture whose burning desire is to throw off the yoke of moral and ethical behavior and wallow in the depths of depravity without having to endure criticism or consequences. It is no accident that this movement was brought into being by the same generation that brought us the sexual revolution, which contributed to an environment in which men assumed that women were always willing to have sex. It produced a president of the United States who, perhaps believing himself to be the reincarnation of John F. Kennedy, assumed that he had the right to use and abuse any woman who caught his eye, thereby saddling an entire generation of parents with the unenviable task of trying to explain the phrase "oral sex" to their young children. Despite the current backlash against the extremes that resulted, the game is still afoot. Here is an example of the hypocrisy of this movement: female athletes recently posed in a sports magazine wearing nothing except "empowering" words written on their bodies. This was supposedly to protest sexual harassment by men. Wait. What? I must be slow. Is the best way to protest the objectification of woman a photo spread that objectifies women? This is an example of the Orwellian mindset pervading our culture. This kind of thinking allows people to promote lies as truth and truth as lies. Women are not empowered by posing nude.

Institutional Christianity is complicit in this to the degree that it seeks to conform to the values and practices of the secular world. The untold millions of dollars churches spend to move to more affluent areas and build state-of-the-art facilities may impress people and draw them in for a time, but churches saddled with massive debt often lack the resources to do much more than maintain the buildings and pay staff. The reasons for moving, while couched in the best possible terms, are not always laudable. I know of a church that was established in a small Midwest community at the end of the nineteenth century as a neighborhood church. Over the years the neighborhood changed as the original members or their descendants moved out and were replaced by African American and Latino residents. The church did little to reach out to their new neighbors, preferring instead to retain their historic ethnic identity. Near the end of the church's life as a unique congregation, someone managed to convince the leadership to open an afterschool program in the church. Some of the long-standing members of the church complained because they did not want "those people" messing up their beautiful building. Eventually the church closed its doors and merged with another congregation in a "better" part of town. They abandoned a wonderful ministry opportunity because their comfort was more important than reaching out to people who were different ethnically and economically.

This is only one example among many. Three other churches did the same thing during my time in that community.

I desperately want to believe that deep down people know what is right; they just cannot find the courage to do it. I know this to be true of myself. It is easier to acquiesce to peer pressure than to publicly stand up for what one knows to be true. The pressure to conform is huge in our culture these days. It sometimes seems like people are walking around with giant chips on their shoulders, looking for reasons to be offended. This is gradually creating an environment in which it is impossible to have an intelligent conversation about climate change, politics, immigration, or gender identity, let alone talking to a stranger about Jesus. We are told that we must simply accept the conclusions of "settled science," conveniently forgetting that at one point in the not-too-distant past it was settled science that the earth was flat and that the sun and planets revolved around it. It is the height of arrogance to suggest that we have reached the pinnacle of human knowledge in any area of science or philosophy. The rock-solid conclusions of today far too often end up being the debunked theories of tomorrow. This is true in every area of human inquiry, including questions about sexual behavior and its relationship to the emotional response we identify as love.

> To see what is right and not do it is want of courage, or of principle.
>
> —Confucius[10]

I find it ironic that the same people who declare that sexual intercourse has nothing to do with love also insist that love is best expressed in a sexual relationship. To wit: I can only truly love someone with whom I am having sex. Sexual intercourse is enjoyable in the proper context, but it is not the be-all and end-all of intimacy, and it is certainly not the purest form of love. The lie we are told to accept as true is that the deepest form of love is sexual. Atheists, agnostics, and hedonists may embrace this idea (pun intended) but there is no conceivable way for faithful followers of Jesus to agree. Love in its highest and truest form transcends the physical, a fact made even more apparent by married couples whose love continues and grows after sexual intimacy is no longer possible or even desired. "'Greater love has no one that this,' Jesus declared, 'that someone lay down his life for his friends.'"[11] Some scholars claim that Jesus was secretly married to Mary Magdalene. The truth is that if he had been married there would have been no reason to suppress the fact because it was a normal part of life in Jesus' time and

10. https://www.azquotes.com/quote/62186.
11. John 15:13.

culture even for rabbis. Conspiracy theorists claim the church knew Jesus was married but suppressed it to support the doctrine of celibacy. This statement is made in ignorance of the fact that priests routinely married during the first three or four centuries of the church's existence and still wed in the Orthodox Church today. I do not believe that conspiracy theorists care if Jesus was married; they just want proof that he had sex outside of marriage so that they can justify their morally bankrupt beliefs and practices. They desperately grasp at any scrap of evidence they can find to make their pronouncements, fabricating it if it does not exist.

What, you may ask, is the evidence for these pronouncements? It was the discovery of a collection of documents, allegedly suppressed by the winning faction in the early church, that present an entirely different picture of Jesus, his life, and his ministry. I am not upset that these documents came to light and were made available in translation to the public. They present a fascinating picture of doctrinal and theological argument in the third and fourth centuries. The problem is that scholars with an agenda want to present them as works that were composed much earlier but were rejected by those in power over the church in favor of the documents that supported their version of the truth. The problems with this theory are myriad, but chief among them is that these documents are written in Greek and represent a thoroughly Greek approach to Jesus. The most reputable scholars have categorically rejected them as works of fiction, but that does not stop those who desire is to rewrite the story of Jesus in a way that supports every kind of aberrant sexual behavior. These scholars claim that they are bravely standing up to the patriarchal and antiquated thinking of the primitive church, but the truth is that their position is a cowardly act designed to allow them to avoid the hard work of living the way Jesus wants his followers to live and to suffer the hatred of the world because of it.

Supporters of the current moral ambiguity of Western culture point to the Greeks and the Romans as examples of times when morality was fluid. While there is some degree of truth to this, the fact is that both these cultures fell disastrously. The decadence of the Romans is cited by historians as one of the main reasons for the demise of their empire. We claim to be more enlightened than the ancients, but that is patently wrong. Some of the most virulent venereal diseases found their way to Europe because explorers and soldiers, good Christians who all believed their actions were just, saw nothing wrong with raping the native women they found in what became known as the Americas. Institutional Christianity looked the other way, caring only for the vast wealth they hoped to accrue to fund their military conquests and territorial ambitions across Europe. Entire civilizations on the American continent were destroyed by diseases nominal Christians visited upon them as they forcibly satisfied their lusts with the native women. Diseases rapidly spread throughout Europe because "Christian" men and women believed it was their right to have sex with whomever they desired regardless of their marital situation. I note with no small amount of sadness that when these diseases emerged the most common response was to seek a medical cure rather than ceasing to engage in the behavior that spread the disease in the first place.

I realize it will be difficult for some readers to understand that I am talking about behaviors, not the people who engage in them. Behaviors can be good, neutral, evil, or some combination of all three, but every behavior has consequences. It is possible (given enough intellectual maturity) to condemn behaviors without condemning those who engage in them. Unfortunately, some people are incapable of separating the two. They demand that their actions be accepted as an essential part of their identity. This is another reason why institutional Christianities are dying. Jesus met people in their sinfulness, accepted them as children of God, and then challenged them to become who and what God intended them to be, which meant setting aside their sinful behavior. Institutional Christianities believe in meeting people where they are, blessing what they choose to do and be, and not challenging them to change in any way except paying lip service to the current version of social justice. This is nothing more or less than cowardice in the name of self-preservation. It is clearly not a winning strategy. People are miserable because they are mired in sin; baptizing sin does not help. Few people will give their lives and resources to an institution that does not challenge them. After all, there are plenty of social and philanthropic organizations that do not require you to get up early on a Sunday morning and attend a lecture accompanied by music performed by amateurs, or, if your church has the resources, paid professionals whose relationship to Jesus is dubious. Young families might attend a church during the school year if their children are entertained while they attend a service that is more like a concert than worship. They will not, however, commit at a level that precludes them from skipping church most of the summer.

> It's my petty fear of personal rejection that allows so many true evils to exist. My cowardice enables atrocities.
>
> —CHUCK PALAHNIUK[12]

Institutional Christians in the West are becoming increasingly secularized, often without realizing or acknowledging it. Some of this is due to peer pressure, but I prefer to identify it mainly as what it is: cowardice. In my

12. https://www.azquotes.com/quote/508121.

experience, church goers will quickly set aside attending worship, participating in a Bible study, or taking part in an important meeting if they are
invited to do something more fun by their non-church friends, or that en-
hances their standing in the community in which they live. This is especially
true when it comes to sporting events at any level. Some churches justify
this by claiming that it is an opportunity for what was called "friendship
evangelism" and urging their members to use it as such but I disagree. I believe that Christians acquiesce in these situations because they do not want
to be labeled as "Bible-thumpers" or "fundamentalists" by those with whom
they spend more than an hour or two each week. Their church relationships
may be important to them, but not important enough for them to bravely
take a stand that might make them unpopular among their colleagues and
neighbors. There are two issues at work here. First, there is the cowardice
that rears its ugly head in the face of the desire to preserve fragile social relationships. Second, there is the dangerous belief that one can take God for
granted, relying on his amazing grace to make up for our abundant short-
comings. While the latter may be true in one sense, taking grace for granted
betrays a faith that does not take God seriously. Grace is free, according to
every reformed definition of the word, but it is not cheap and must not be
used as an excuse for a lack of commitment.

Another form of cowardice in the name of self-preservation can be
observed among those church goers who socialize only with other church
goers, preferably those in the same social and economic class. It may seem
unfair to characterize this as cowardice, but I am applying it to myself as
well. Some of our reticence is due in part to the prevailing cultural notion
that all religions are equally valid and that any attempt to "evangelize"
one's non-Christian neighbors, colleagues, and friends is intolerant. While
it is true that the forms of evangelism used in the 1970s are no longer effective in the West, there are ways to have conversations with people that
can open doors to understanding and, perhaps, conversion. We need to
be sensitive about it, but we must never compromise our belief that faith
in Jesus provides the promise and assurance of a place in eternity that no
other religion offers. This is becoming increasingly difficult in a culture
where hostility to Christianity is rapidly growing and becoming socially
unacceptable. I once had a conversation with a Christian employee at a
large international corporation who was told to stop inviting people to
participate in a religious retreat in which he was involved because it was
a violation of company policy. He agreed to the restriction rather than
lose his well-paid job. There is a fine line between self-preservation and
cowardice, but the time is coming when that line will be broader. It will
mean making a choice between faithfulness and accommodation.

The sad truth is that atheists, agnostics, and haters of all things religious will always distrust anyone with a connection to anything that smacks of belief in something other than achievement of a utopian civilization purely through human effort and achievement. The worst part about this is that institutional Christianities have defected to the camp of the enemy, believing that the future of the church depends upon adapting to prevailing cultural beliefs. It is not having the desired result. A 2015 Pew Research Center reported that mainline Protestant churches lost five million members between 2007 and 2015.[13] This despite adherence to the advice of liberal academicians, intellectuals, and theologians that they abandon traditional styles of worship and interpretations of the Bible to better attract people in these changing times. Albert Einstein is reputed to have defined insanity as the act of doing the same thing repeatedly and expecting a different result. Institutional Christianities that are more conservative are doing marginally better but still struggling. Non-denominational mega-churches grow and survive for a time by finding ways to attract huge crowds of people without requiring a huge personal commitment. All continue to stubbornly believe that the solution is to be a better institution, not to find a different way of being the church. The truth is that the institution needs to die because it is consuming energy and resources better spent on helping lost and hurting people in the world. One time when Jesus was visiting Jerusalem with his disciples, they made sure he noticed the magnificently ornate temple complex Herod had built to appease the Jews. Jesus told them that the time would soon come when the building would be destroyed.[14] They were appalled by the thought, but the truth is that the destruction of the temple did not stall or stop either Judaism or the movement that became Christianity.

Self-preservation requires compromise and institutional Christianity is adept at it, but it has not helped stem the hemorrhaging of members. Cowardice in the face of criticism is displayed in the unwillingness to take a stand against the assertion that there is no stand everyone should be required to take as a matter of faith. The problem is not the claim that only one set of beliefs is true; it is the claim that every set of beliefs is equally true. The notion that unity is only found in diversity is nonsense. It is an example of Orwellian doublespeak. Jesus spoke about unity of purpose and vision, all the while emphasizing that hitherto disparate groups could come together

---

13. Lipka, Michael. "Mainline Protestants make up shrinking number of U.S. adults." *Fact Tank* (blog), *Pew Research Center*, May 18, 2015, https://www.pewresearch.org/fact-tank/2015/05/18/mainline-protestants-make-up-shrinking-number-of-u-s-adults/.

14. Then Jesus asked him, "Do you see these great buildings? Not one stone will be left here upon another; all will be thrown down" (Mark 13:2).

around a common focus. The early church followed this example, at least for a short while, but the all-too-human propensity to divide into classes based on wealth, social standing, and ethnicity soon reared its ugly head. There is no unity in diversity; there is only division.

Chapter 12

There is *No* Unity in Diversity

> My concern is that our religions, the diversity of our religious doctrines, is going to get us killed. I'm worried that our religious discourse—our religious beliefs are ultimately incompatible with civilization.
>
> —Sam Harris[1]

One claim progressive institutional Christianities make is that unity is found in diversity. This is a smokescreen designed to obscure their agenda. The unity they advocate is Orwellian because while they profess to believe that every religion, ideology, viewpoint, and opinion is equally valid, the only views they accept are those that conform to their agenda. There can be unity of purpose despite differing beliefs, but it is impossible to reconcile diametrically opposed doctrinal and theological assertions. Some Christians reject the validity of Judaism based on the belief that Christianity supplanted and replaced it. Judaism rejects Christianity as heretical based on assertions Christians make concerning Jesus' divine nature. Islam accepts that Judaism and Christianity contain truth but asserts without apology that both religions have been supplanted by the corrective teaching of Mohammed in the Qur'an. Mormons claim that Joseph Smith received a divine revelation that corrected Judaism, Christianity, and Islam. Hindus, Taoists, Neo-pagans, agnostics and atheists all claim that if there is objective, absolute truth, they alone possess it. The obvious question: Is everyone right or is everyone wrong? Wars have been fought and lives destroyed in the effort to answer that question.

Fundamentalist elements in every religion claim to have a lock on the truth. The problem is not the claim, but the lengths to which they go to

1. https://www.brainyquote.com/quotes/sam_harris_527718.

defend the validity of their assertions. These types of disagreements in the earliest communities of Jesus followers, while often heated, did not often move beyond the bounds of rhetoric. Excommunication meant refusal to celebrate the Eucharist (communion) with one's theological opponents. This changed when the victors at the Council of Nicaea declared those on the losing side heretics and demanded that Constantine strip them of their positions and exile them in the name of establishing and promoting religious unity in the empire. Everyone soon realized that it was possible to vanquish one's theological opponents by the simple expedient of winning the emperor's favor. This resulted in excesses of oppression that have reverberated down through the halls of history into the present day, which is problematic given that there is no record of Jesus condoning any kind of violence when proclaiming or defending his message. There are so many examples of how Christianities have violated this in the past that it is difficult to choose one to illustrate the point. It may be enough to speak generally.

Doctrinal disputes among the first organized communities of Jesus followers were limited in the earliest years of the church's existence because of several factors, among them persecution and the effective autonomy of groups that were widely spread across Asia Minor and the Near East. Despite what the Roman Catholic Church and its defenders may claim, Rome did not gain comprehensive doctrinal supremacy over Christian communities in the western Roman Empire until well into the sixth century. It never had any significant influence in the churches of the Eastern Empire, although it vociferously claimed otherwise. East and West were partners at times, but never really unified in doctrine and belief. This was not major problem until Nicaea. The theological and doctrinal divisions between Eastern and Western Catholicism have been around since the earliest days of Christianity and continue to the present day. One could argue that Eastern Christianity, deeply rooted in places like Alexandria, Cappadocia, and Syria, has a greater claim to authenticity than does Western Christianity, being a form of the faith that, while influenced by Greek philosophy, retains vestiges of the ancient beliefs about Jesus. It is likely that the earliest followers of Jesus would recognize some of what the East has historically believed. Any serious attempt to uncover the earliest layer of belief needs to begin not in the archives of the West, but in those of the East. Constantinople is of more help to us in this endeavor than Rome. Institutional Christianities in the West will be well-served if they are willing to set aside their claims to doctrinal or theological authority and sit once more at the feet of Jesus in his Jewish context. His preaching and teaching are best understood within the context of the Eastern, not the Western way of viewing reality. The only chance institutional Christianity has of experiencing true reformation is by setting aside long-held and deeply entrenched beliefs about what it means to be the church. It will require Christianity to redefine much of what it believes about Jesus, the gospel, unity, and, perhaps most uncomfortable of all, tolerance. Human nature being what it is, this will not be an easy task.

In the practice of tolerance, one's enemy is the best teacher.

—DALAI LAMA XIV[2]

"Unity in diversity" is only one of the absurd statements that the pompous pronouncers of doublespeak regularly make. Self-proclaimed enlightened ones rule the day in every corner of western culture, including institutional Christianity. Anyone daring to challenge the prevailing narrative is subjected to volleys of faux outrage, ad hominem attacks and vile profanity, if not physical attack. The most vocal proponents of tolerance stridently denounce and refuse to tolerate those who openly oppose their viewpoint. Those who loudly call for unity simultaneously demand, without any apparent sense of irony, complete separation from and persecution of those who hold beliefs they deem unacceptable. The loudest and most heated protests issue forth from college campuses, whose young inhabitants apparently believe that their opinions carry more weight than the knowledge and experience of the generations who have gone before them. It is tragic that so many institutions of higher learning have become little more than reeducation camps designed to tell students what to think instead of teaching them how to think. Seminaries are increasingly finding ways to provide free education to those entering the ministry. Efforts are afoot to provide "free college education for all," even though not everyone is cut out for college. Nothing is free, of course, and is little doubt that the price of a "free" education is forced adherence to the ideological agenda of the institution. In the secular world, enrollments are steadily dropping at some of the most prestigious schools in response to reports of blatant bias and censorship of views deemed unacceptable. Theological schools struggle as well in the face of a rapidly decreasing number of churches looking for pastors. How sad it is, too, that the elders of our culture allow themselves to be schooled by children, many of whom have never experienced anything even approaching true adversity. Professors whose responsibility is to challenge our youth as they enter adulthood instead find themselves cowed into submission to the culture of accommodation by the threat of attacks on social media and by the real possibility of losing their jobs.

The clamorous cries for unity and tolerance have ironically done much to divide our culture into ever smaller groups focused on their own agenda and interests all, ironically, in the name of making our society stronger.

2. https://www.brainyquote.com/quotes/dalai_lama_158918.

Actions that used to be considered hateful segregation are now touted as sensitive and empowering. Groups demand their own "safe spaces" on campuses, their own places to congregate, and special recognition by society for their causes. Ethnic groups demand that they be provided with designated spaces where they can associate with their own kind, something that was forced upon German Americans during the American Revolution, African Americans in the post-Civil War, and South and Japanese Americans during the Second World War, to give just a few examples. I recently heard of one university, no doubt in response to rising criticism, that decided to create a safe space for white students. Doublespeak is alive and well in academia!

The call for unity in diversity is obviously not limited to any one sphere. Pundits across the political spectrum may be divided by their ideology, but almost all of them agree that the United States of America is far from united. They stress the clear and present political divisions in our country during every election cycle, which cycles seem to grow longer and longer every year. They act like this is something new, but the reality is that we have never been completely unified or united as a country. Oh, there have been moments when the country was more united than divided, to be sure, but there has never been complete unity among every citizen at any given moment if the historical record is to be trusted. For instance, those who called the territories that became the United States of America home in its earliest days were hardly of one mind concerning its future. France, Spain, and England each laid claim to large tracts of land, based in part on the proclamation of a dead pope who never set foot on the continent but who nonetheless believed he had the authority to divide the newly discovered lands among the powers of Europe without any concern for those who were already living there. Let us please not forget those unfortunate inhabitants who had settled the continent long before Europeans took notice. If those we now call Native Americans had united against the threat of European invasion instead of using Europeans to settle their disputes with other tribes, we would be living in a different world.

While the United States may not be as deeply divided along political lines as some would have us believe, there are some clear and profound divisions. The gap between rich and poor seems to be widening as the middle class shrinks. Then there is a clear ideological divide between those who believe that government control over its citizens should be limited and those who believe that government should be responsible for spending everyone's money on their behalf and taking care of their every basic need. Trust of those in authority is low. Communities on the coasts distrust the people in the middle of the country and vice-versa. Successive generations resent the fact that they seem to have fewer opportunities to attain the level of success achieved by their parents. Misuse and abuse of the social welfare system has created entire communities dependent on government guidance; our nation is on the verge of revolution. It is always possible, of course, that we will pull ourselves back from the brink of the abyss before it is too late. Institutional Christianities could speak into this, if only they were willing to demonstrate how to put unity of purpose and the value of compassionate community ahead of doctrinal, political, or ideological conformity.

> Human beings will be happier—not when they cure cancer or get to Mars or eliminate racial prejudice or flush Lake Erie but when they find ways to inhabit primitive communities again. That's my utopia.
>
> —KURT VONNEGUT[3]

The concept of utopia is, by definition, utopian. It presumes that humanity can attain a level of unity that will enable it to build a perfect society. Given human nature, this is naïve, as naïve as suggesting that there has ever been a time in the history of the world when human society has not been fragmented to some degree. Numerous attempts have been made throughout history to unite sizeable portions of humanity into a single empire or nation, but none of them lasted longer than a few centuries at best. Every effort at creating a utopia ended in failure. Utopias are doomed to failure for one simple reason: they are formulated, created, managed, and inhabited by people. This is as true in the religious as it is in the secular realm. Humanity seems to be incapable of setting aside self-interest to achieve something good, let alone something great. Communism and socialism are laudable concepts, but basic human greed prevents them from being fully realized as viable forms of social organization. Egalitarianism is a noble idea but will never be fully realized; people cannot seem to resist the urge to exercise control over others. They may go to significant effort to preserve the appearance of equality by providing everyone else with just enough to survive while amassing power and wealth for a small elite. Equality, as it is practically expressed these days, is not true equality. As George Orwell put it in his novel *Animal Farm*, "All animals are equal, but some animals are more equal than others."[4]

This may be true in secular society, but should it be true in the church as the visible expression of the body of Christ? There is ample evidence that Jesus expected his followers to build a unified, egalitarian community that placed hands-on service ahead of institutional or social status. He made

---

3. https://www.brainyquote.com/quotes/kurt_vonnegut_135186.
4. https://www.brainyquote.com/quotes/george_orwell_100005.

numerous statements to this effect, declaring that his followers should wash one another's feet following his example,[5] an expression of humbleness and service, whether taken literally or not.[6] Jesus certainly knew that his followers would struggle to maintain unity; his last spoken prayer is a fervent plea that his followers would be united in every possible way.[7] Despite all the rosy pictures to the contrary, any real sense of unity among the followers of Jesus died with the first generation of believers. The first few generations of Jesus followers often had all they could do just to survive in the face of sporadic persecution at the hands of religious and secular authorities. It is also important to understand that dissension and division increasingly plagued the church after the leaders in Jerusalem, perhaps reluctantly, decided that non-Jews could become full followers of Jesus without converting to Judaism. Factionalism was already present, but if you want to see it at its most virulent, spend some time reading and studying the letters that Paul wrote to the faith community in Corinth.

While no one can come up with a verifiable number, there are obviously many different denominations, churches, and other expressions of Christianity in the world.[8] The real issue in this is not the actual number, but the fact that the divisions exist at all.[9] One of the accusations leveled against the validity of Christianity is that the proliferation of groups expressing different beliefs while claiming to be the only ones who have the truth cast doubt among non-believers on the entire Christian message. Some claim that every expression of Christianity is true in its own way, but that is less probable than the statement that none are right. To utilize a phrase of which my father is fond, "That's just stupid." Rather than owning up to the fact that the existence of so many groups making contradictory claims is a problem, apologists seek excuses for why multiple churches and denominations is a good thing. I recently heard someone sincerely declare that denominational differences are based on differences of opinion, not different beliefs. Intentionally or not, he was attempting to paint a utopian

5. "So if I, your Lord and Teacher, have washed your feet, you also ought to wash one another's feet" (John 13:14).

6. The institutional church might be in a better place today if it had taken the advice of some of the Reformers and made foot-washing a sacrament.

7. John 17.

8. Some estimate as many as forty thousand different denominations and churches, but this number is vigorously disputed by many scholars.

9. Full disclosure: I write this as one who grew up Roman Catholic and then willingly became Presbyterian, which traces its roots back to the Protestant Reformation. I subsequently left the Presbyterian denomination in which I was ordained and joined a new one. I would likely be declared heretic by all of them today.

picture of Christianity as unified despite its obvious divisions. With all due respect, I must respond that this is simply not true. This may be how we want to view it today, but the reality is that most Christian sects and denominations were born in bloodshed to proclaim and defend deeply held beliefs that differed from those of the status quo. Perhaps I am being naïve, but I strongly suspect that part of the proliferation of churches and denominations has to do with the fact that few people these days are willing to suffer or die for an opinion—they would rather just gather up their toys and go find another place to play.

If denominationalism was truly based solely on different opinions about nonessential issues such as, for instance, worship style or music preferences, it would not necessarily be detrimental to the church's mission; it could, in fact, be beneficial. One problem is that what one group may consider nonessential, another group characterizes as uncompromisingly essential. One example is baptism. Some will insist, pointing to evidence from the Bible, that baptism be restricted to those who are old enough to understand its significance and intentionally request it. Others, using both biblical evidence and tradition, insist that it is perfectly acceptable to baptize infants; some, in fact, will insist that failure to do so will result in the infant being barred from heaven if he or she dies before baptism. Some insist that baptism is only valid if the one being baptized is fully immersed in water. Others declare with equal insistence that any amount of water is enough, the symbolism of the act being more important than the quantity of water used. Speaking of quantity, countless gallons of blood have been spilled defending one view over another. Anabaptists were vigorously persecuted because they had the audacity to insist that only adults who had made a profession of faith could be baptized. They claimed that baptism was important but not necessary for salvation because Jesus did not explicitly make it a prerequisite. Baptism is an important ritual, but anyone who reads the words of the Bible with integrity cannot fail to agree that it must never be viewed as a means of attaining salvation. Why, then, should one group of Christians persecute another group simply because they disagree about the efficacy of a ritual? Frankly, while infant baptisms are cute, they are meaningless in any significant and eternal sense. Baptism does not convey eternal salvation. It is a statement of faith at best, not some kind of magical conveyance of a spiritual benefit. Why would God place such power in the hands of sinful, fallible human beings?

> Sheer scholarship alone cannot reveal to us the gospel of grace. We must never allow the authority of books, institutions, or leaders to replace the authority of knowing Jesus Christ

personally and directly. When the religious views of others interpose between us and the primary experience of Jesus as the Christ, we become un–convicted and unpersuasive travel agents handing out brochures to places we have never visited.

—BRENNAN MANNING[10]

Christianity must unify if it is to successfully carry out the mission with which Jesus entrusted it. This is *not* a solitary endeavor; it is designed to be practiced in community with other believers. But institutions are not necessarily communities. I have never been part of a church that was not fragmented. We may hide behind a façade of a common mission, vision, and purpose statement, but the unvarnished truth is that the church where everyone is 100 percent in agreement is as rare as hen's teeth. Divisions exist whenever humans form groups of any kind, religious or otherwise. Christianity is egalitarian, but rare is the congregation that is not intentionally or unintentionally segregated according race, class, or income. This is one reason why institutional Christianities are diseased and dying. Faith is the unmediated experience of Jesus as one's personal Savior, not assent to institutionally approved doctrines of dubious, and sometimes harmful, spiritual value. I once belonged to a denomination that actively promoted racial diversity as a higher value than biblical or doctrinal integrity even in those regions where achieving racial diversity was impossible given the racial homogeneity of the community. The result was that any church that promoted biblical values above racial diversity was ostracized.

One of the most popular activities these days is accusing people of racism and bigotry, often on the flimsiest of evidence. Like the story of the boy who cried wolf, accusations of racism have lost their power because they have been overused. Besides this, the truth, one we are desperately unwilling to admit, is that, depending on how you choose to define the terms, everyone is racist or bigoted. Think about it: when given the choice between associating with people like you and people who are different, whom will you be most inclined to approach? I have witnessed people being shunned or ignored in every church of which I have been a part simply because they looked different or did not fit into the dominant social culture of the church. One example stands out: There was an individual at a church I served as a student intern during my seminary training who had social and intellectual challenges. The congregation took pride in their effort to welcome him but avoided sitting with him during the social hour or at potlucks because his hygiene habits and table manners were undesirable. I sat with him because I was embarrassed by how he was treated, not because I was spiritually superior. Another

10. https://www.azquotes.com/quote/487590.

church I served held a dinner every Wednesday evening during the program year at which people were encouraged to socialize with people they did not know and form new relationships. Every week without fail the same people sat together, and the same socially challenged people were ignored and sat alone unless no other seats were available for latecomers. The people who most were vocal in their criticism of the church for its failure to care for strangers also routinely ignored those they deemed too strange to warrant friendship or fellowship. I often found myself sitting with "the least of these, my brothers,"[11] not so much because I was especially pious, but because I was embarrassed at how the least desirable members of the church were being treated by people who should have known and who claimed to know better.

One community in which I served as a pastor was segregated not so much by conscious choice as by circumstances of geography and demographics. The church campus was on the north end of town, a long way away from the poverty-stricken, largely African American, Hispanic, and Asian south end. The handful of non-Caucasians, with a few exceptions, were children adopted mostly from other countries. One family made the heroic decision to adopt African American children from the community, for which they are to be commended. Others adopted children from China, Vietnam, Africa, and other impoverished countries. Nonetheless, I heard a lot of talk about how we needed to help "those people," but never encountered anyone willing to move into the communities where they lived. My family and I were one of the few households that lived within easy walking distance of the poorer sections of town, not because we had a choice but because we did not have the financial resources to live in the upper-class sections of town. In all fairness, I did not do much to reach out to that community apart from briefly serving on the board of an organization that gave me the opportunity to make connections with churches in that part of town. I was unsuccessful because I was busy with my responsibilities at the church I served and because the churches in the poor sections of town did not trust the motives of the "rich white folk" in the more affluent parts of the community. We make lots of noise about caring for the poor, but how many of us are willing to move into those areas of town and be present with those in need?

When you get right down to it, people naturally, probably unconsciously, gravitate toward those to whom they can relate and avoid those who are not in the same social class or economic level. Because of this, institutional Christianity is fragmented, and it is difficult to find authentic unity, although examples do exist. In general, however, large churches shun and look down on small churches, and small churches resent the large

11. Matt 25:31–46.

ones. Rich churches shun poor ones within the same denomination and the same community. People shun people in the same congregation based on class and social standing, while simultaneously bemoaning the divisions in church and society and the lack of diversity in the church. The churches' (both large and small) solution is to create mission, vision, and purpose statements, but most of them are little more than jingoistic attempts to assuage the consciences of those who want to pay lip service to the gospel while maintaining their preferred level of comfort. This sounds harsh, but it is based on personal experience serving on the front lines of ministry. Vision and purpose statements become little more than propaganda aimed at creating a sense of unity where none exists. They are an attempt to manufacture unity in a culture that promotes division. The primary blame for this does not rest with the local congregation or its members. Instead, denominational pundits at the national level, some of whom have little or no experience in the field, push expensive programs and clever strategies that look good on paper, but rarely produce the desired results. We want there to be unity in diversity, and we are sure we can achieve it with the right program, but time and again those pesky societal divisions get in the way. We want people who are different to come to us, and then we want them to change so that they can be like us. We claim to want unity in diversity, but we do everything possible to promote division.

Here is the problem: There is no unity in diversity, at least not in the way it is defined and promoted today. It is a unity in diversity that requires one to accept the validity of the position that the only valid belief is the belief that there are no universally valid beliefs. This is classic Orwellian doublespeak. While it may be a noble sentiment, it simply does not work in the real world because it is not really aimed at achieving unity of purpose. The "unity in diversity" argument, as employed by it most vocal proponents, is a wolf in sheep's clothing. It requires that one hold two completely opposing beliefs in tension to maintain the appearance of unity not for the sake of promoting the truth but for the sole purpose of garnering financial support for the institution. The practical result is that this makes the truth relative, at best, reducing it to the status of an opinion. The fundamental problem is that no two opposing facts can be equally true. While it is possible, and perhaps even desirable, to maintain unity despite differences over nonessentials, it is impossible to maintain unity when the differences involve essential matters of faith and belief. Unfortunately, even distinguishing between essential and nonessential issues has become subjective. There no longer seems to be a core belief around which Christians are willing to unite. The uncomfortable fact is that those in power do not really believe that there can be unity in diversity; they simply want those who disagree to be quiet, go along with the program, and give their money to the institution.

I have seen this play out more times than I want to remember. I spent more than two decades watching as the liberal/progressive wing of the denomination in which I was ordained gradually took over all the positions of power, in part because the conservative and evangelical churches did not want to waste time and resources focusing on politics. I was complicit in this failure to take notice and act. When evangelicals finally realized what was happening, it was too late. The progressive wing had already whittled away at traditional beliefs even as they scrupulously avoided seeking to officially change them. They emphasized what they believed would allow them to promote a social agenda that was in keeping with the words of Jesus, while slowly pushing aside the historic doctrines they rejected. All the while, they encouraged what they characterized as debate, but which was a carefully choreographed effort to stifle any opposition to the progressive position. Draconian laws aimed at maintaining financial control over individual congregations meant that some churches were unable to leave a denomination increasingly at odds with the beliefs of many of its members.

Once it became apparent that some of the largest churches in the denomination were willing to leverage financial resources to fight a costly legal battle over the issue of separation, some of the leaders in the lower governing bodies began to see the wisdom of making concessions, although they were afraid to push too hard against the official position. One common plea directed toward congregations that desired separation was "We need your voice" in discussions about doctrine and practice. This may have been sincere on the part of some, but at the national level it was the height of hypocrisy. Directives were issued from the highest level of church government that any congregation seeking separation was required to surrender its property to the denomination or purchase it at its appraised value. Some congregations acquiesced, but others sought redress in the secular courts. In my opinion, neither side acted with complete spiritual integrity. The demand for financial compensation conveniently ignored the fact most of the congregations held title to their property long before they entered the denomination. The denominational officials appealed to a clause added to church polity in the 1980s, long after most churches had been founded. On the other side of the conflict, if congregations really believed they were taking the high ground doctrinally and theologically, they would have abandoned their property and kept following Jesus' mission without it. Jesus is not glorified in any way by the rancor, wrangling, and financial dealing that has and is still taking place. This is happening in other denominations as well, to the detriment of Jesus' mission.

The claim is made that Christians, regardless of their specific beliefs, are part of what is called the "body of Christ." If this is true, then the body is afflicted with leprosy, cancer, and every other kind of fatal illness. Institutional Christianities are their own worst enemies. This is demonstrated in the kind of public pronouncements denominational officials choose to make when they wade into secular issues. Declarative statements by religious leaders about "climate change" (a scientific, not a religious concern) bring ridicule on Christianity if they are not made in the context of stewardship of creation, which is a biblical mandate. Political statements from religious leaders about politicians make Christians look ludicrous and do not help bring about real change. Followers of Jesus have no business trying to tie politics to religion. Politics will not save anyone. In fact, the overwhelming testimony of history is that it will lead only to despair and destruction. The truth is that the body of Christ is not an institution, nor was it ever intended to be. It is a group of people coalesced and united around a common belief and purpose and, most importantly, a person named Jesus: the only person who gives the church any meaning. Any denomination that devotes resources to maintaining a lobbying office in Washington DC is not helping the body of Christ grow. Jesus' mission was focused on changing people, not on changing institutions or formulating new laws and policies.

The way to get beyond this is to understand that when Jesus prayed for the unity of his followers he was not praying for the unity of an institution. Nothing unites the disparate groups who claim to be Christian apart from the belief that they are spiritually connected to Jesus, who was called the Christ (Messiah) by his followers, and who preached a message of love and acceptance. The proliferation of Christianities, some of them so different as to call into question whether there is anything so quintessential as a set of core Christian beliefs, brings disrepute upon the cause of Christ. Any truly useful set of core beliefs must focus on Jesus' message, not on doctrines about Jesus. Christians the world over will argue vociferously over this, but one need only go back to the words of Jesus to discover the truth. Of course, this requires setting aside presuppositions that are many centuries old in some cases. I do not believe that Jesus died so that his followers could create an institution. The atrocities committed in the name of Jesus in the past, as well as the lies promoted in his name today, convince me that the leprous, cancer-filled, multi-headed beast that calls itself institutional Christianity is doomed to die. The good news is that something far better will take its place.

Institutions try to enforce unity but are incapable of creating more than a pale imitation of it. Unity is based on a commonality of belief and purpose. The first generation of Jesus followers embodied this in the desire to die for him as he had died for them. The faith of that generation is on full display in the writings from the earliest years of the Jesus movement. Imagine how the current crop of institutional church leaders might respond if they were convicted of the crime of being Christians and condemned to die by being killed and consumed by lions. My guess is that many of them would renounce their faith rather than die. How many of them, I wonder, would respond as did Ignatius, a bishop of Antioch in the first century? While on his way to Rome for the above-mentioned method of execution, he wrote to the faith community there to tell them not to try to save him, dying for Christ being the greatest goal of a believer in those days.[12]

Faithful followers of Jesus outside of the Western world will resonate with the words of dedicated people like Ignatius. Those who claim to be followers of Jesus in the West believe that it is enough to sacrifice a little comfort, but rarely consider what it might mean to sacrifice their lives. The first few generations of Jesus followers rushed gladly toward death, knowing that it was nothing more than a doorway to eternal life and that the manner of their demise would bring others to faith in him. Many of those who claim to be the spiritual descendants of those first faithful followers avoid inconvenience, let alone death, at all costs, limping toward oblivion instead of considering what it means to live and die for Jesus and act accordingly.

12. Ignatius of Antioch's letter to the Romans can be read at http://www.newadvent. org/fathers/0107.htm.

Chapter 13

Limping Toward Oblivion

> I am ashamed to think how easily we capitulate to badges and names, to large societies and dead institutions.
>
> —Ralph Waldo Emerson[1]

It is easy to slip into generalities when undertaking to analyze and critique a concept like institutionalism. If I have not made it clear by now, the phrase "institutional Christianities" does not encompass every organized group of Christians. My focus is on institutional expressions of Christianity that have become (intentionally or not) more focused on self-preservation than on carrying out Jesus' mission. Self-preservation is not entirely bad, but it can lead to a compromise of values, beliefs, and practices that is deadly to the institution's purpose. Institutions built by human beings are neither static nor eternal; they have an expiration date. While they can and should change, adapt, and grow over time, it should never be assumed they will be around forever. At some point the institution will outlive its purpose and become so ineffective that reform is no longer enough to fix the problems that beset it. Instead, it needs to die so that something new can take its place. It is better if this is intentional rather than imposed from the outside.

There is plenty of empirical evidence to prove that institutional Christianities in the West are increasingly struggling to remain effective in a rapidly changing cultural environment. The responses vary but can be boiled down to three. First, some churches, pastors, and denominations respond by conforming to cultural values even when they contradict the basic assertions of the Bible concerning faithful obedience to God in the effort to bring in new members. Second, others respond by trying to revive the intellectual

1.https://www.goodreads.com/quotes/259134-i-am-ashamed-to-think-how-easily-we-capitulate-to.

faith of the Reformation and appealing to potential converts by means of carefully reasoned logical arguments and thoughtful propositions. Third, some churches dig in and cling to ancient beliefs and practices without regard for the cultural changes taking place. While each of these methods can result in short-term growth, the harsh reality is that most of the membership growth congregations experience in the West comes from people who leave one church to join another. Few and far between are legitimate conversions of those who have no connection whatsoever to religion. I do not have empirical evidence to prove this, but my experience over three decades of ministry in four different communities backs up the assertion. Mainline churches tended to share their sheep among one another with Pentecostal and independent churches picking up the disaffected members who made the rounds of the traditional churches in the community and finally gave up. A few mainline churches receive members by reaffirmation of faith without requiring much more than attendance at a new member class or classes. Other churches, mainline and independent, insist on public confession of faith, doctrinal examination, and rebaptism based on their belief that they are the only true Christians in the community. Be it lackadaisical or legalistic, both approaches entirely miss the point: Jesus' message rejects both doctrine and rituals as the means of attaining salvation.

Institutional Christianities have developed over time into something far different from the organic faith movement that the apostle Paul describes as the body of Christ. Jesus spent little time talking about the church as such, but he made it clear that his followers were to be an organic community, not an institution. This may seem like a distinction without relevance, but it is vital to the argument I have been making. The church as defined by Jesus and implemented by the first generation of his followers was a group in which people lived in community with one another, meeting in homes for study and public spaces for prayer and worship. They practiced their faith in full view of the world, only going underground during times of intense persecution. Even then, they found ways to meet, gathering secretly in catacombs and cemeteries where they nonetheless faced arrest, imprisonment, torture, and death. This is where the church is supposed to be: on the front line of the struggle, not bivouacked in the back out of harm's way, waiting for others to do the dangerous work. I have watched as churches abandoned their buildings in rundown sections of the city to move out into the affluent areas. In only one case was the church honest about their reason for moving. They admitted that did not want the people in the surrounding neighborhood messing up their building, moving from a poor area of town into a middle-class neighborhood in the hope that it would help them grow. After they relocated to a better section of the city, they started a preschool

program designed to attract a clientele more economically and racially desirable to the powers-that-be, but they have lost more members than they
have gained. This is at least partially because they have adopted a radically
liberal approach to Christianity that does not sit well with those who have
the money to support the institution.

I wish I was making this up. I wish I had done more than grumble
under my breath as I watched churches abandon vital ministry fields among
the poor and needy to build huge modern campuses in affluent areas in
the name of better positioning themselves for service. What I find particularly sad is how quickly and easily people buy into the theory that moving a
church into a growing area will help the church grow. That is true in a sense,
but not the most important one. It may help a church grow by building a
fine new structure with all the latest technology, but what it feels like to
those who are left behind is abandonment. Let us be honest; for mainline
Protestant churches it is as often about "white flight" as anything else. They
may claim they want to help the poor, but they typically want to do it at a
distance to avoid getting their hands dirty. This is a direct consequence of
the institutional mindset, one focused on programs at the expense of really
caring for people. While it is true that Jesus declared that there will always
be poor people, he did not give his followers a pass from the obligation of
physically caring for the those in need, even seeming to imply that entrance
into heaven depended upon it. Quibble all you want about what this means,
and many have, but two points are clear: First, our actions matter to Jesus.
Second, Jesus decides what matters.

While I am aware that institutional Christianity has done much good
in the world, I also know that it has aggravated human suffering through
the centuries and across the world for reasons totally opposed to what Jesus
intended his followers to do in carrying out his mission. The problem for
many people is that they equate Christianity with the institutions that claim
to be announcing the message of Jesus to the world. Some will argue that institutions are necessary to the completion of Jesus' mission. I disagree. First,
institutions are human-created structures that are as effective or ineffective
as the people who lead them. Second, regardless of the reasons for which
they were originally formed, institutions invariably put self-preservation
ahead of working toward the reason for which they came into being. Finally,
while institutional Christianities may serve some purpose in the world, they
are temporal constructs, not eternal creations. Jesus died to save humanity, not to preserve fallible institutions led by fallible people. Those who are
invested in institutional Christianity will disagree precisely because they are
invested in it. This is the inherent danger in institutions. They may start out
with the best and noblest of intentions and a strong to desire to financially

and spiritually invest in others, but they inevitably face the temptation to invest more in the institution in the name of helping it than to invest in people. This is a vicious circle, one that can be solved by holding lightly to the institution and tightly to the purpose for which it was formed.

Self-preservation should be the least and last concern of Christians and the institutions they create in the name of carrying out Jesus' mission. Death is inevitable, only to be feared by those who have no hope of eternal life. This is especially true for followers of Jesus. Remember: The world was not saved by someone who avoided death but by someone who willingly died and whom God willingly raised from the dead. It is abundantly clear from the words of Jesus that the church will suffer violent persecution in what he called the last days as Christians are pressured to give into the demands of the world and publicly repudiate their faith in Jesus. How tragic it is, therefore, that institutional Christianities instead increasingly look for ways to acquiesce to the values of the world, perhaps hoping to avoid persecution, or at least discomfort. The first few generations of Jesus followers experienced varying persecution depending on the local conditions where they lived. Although persecution was sporadic, it was pervasive enough to force the church to focus on surviving and bringing new people into the fold rather than on developing and insisting on strict adherence to a collection of doctrines.

The problem is not so much that institutional Christianity is shrinking as much as it is that its skewed presentation of the gospel has rendered it irrelevant except as another social club for the older generations or a childcare service for young parents. The tragedy is that the message Jesus preached is relevant in every time and culture, but it has been dismissed as outdated and irrelevant in the present by those who claim to be followers of Jesus! The biggest crime perpetrated by institutional Christianities is the promotion and spread of the pernicious lie that God loves you just the way you are and does not want *you* to change unless you disagree with the assertion that you are free to adopt whatever lifestyle or self-identity you desire, regardless of how physically, emotionally, or psychologically harmful it may be. Jesus healed the sick, the lame, the mute, and the blind while calling them from the darkness of despair into the light of hope. Jesus even called them from death to life. The stated aim of institutional Christianities may be to do just that, but it is an Orwellian aim because what they really want to do is keep people in the darkness and use them to further their own agenda. In their view the only way to feel affirmed is to join a community that blames your struggle on others rather than offering you ways to move beyond it. Tolerance is, apparently, more important than transformation. Despite every claim to the contrary, I fail to find any support for this in the words of Jesus. Transformation takes place when I willingly acknowledge that I *need* to change. Progressives insist that the best way to bring people closer to God is by declaring that God loves them just as they are because he made them the way they are and does not want them to change, but deep down inside most people realize this is untrue. Growth does not mean remaining unchanged. A fulfilled life is dynamic, not static. True growth comes through willingness to change, not insistence on remaining the same. A tolerant church offers little hope for real, authentic growth. A transformative church offers not only the possibility of growth, which can be painful, but also hope that growth can be achieved.

> They say a person needs just three things to be truly happy in this world: someone to love, something to do, and something to hope for.
>
> —TOM BODETT[2]

Institutional Christianities that offer uncritical tolerance instead of concrete opportunity for vital transformation are slowly limping towards oblivion. They offer lifeless assertions, not lively challenges. They claim to want to introduce people to Jesus, but it is not the Jesus we meet in the Bible. Institutional Christianities are placing adherence to fluid doctrine above faithful devotion to Jesus. They seem to have forgotten that hope is found in the context of a relationship, not in subscription to doctrines, rules, or rituals. This is not new, being as good a summation as any of Jesus' teaching regarding the burdensome requirements religious leaders were placing on people who only wanted to know that someone with the power to improve their circumstances cared about their struggles. Is this not what we want today? We are feverishly looking for something. The increasingly dismal halls of the internet are filled with people pitifully trying to "go viral" by posting pictures and videos of themselves engaged in foolish, if not outright stupid and dangerous, actions. We elect and support leaders who claim to care about our needs and the issues nearest and dearest to our hearts, only to be disappointed when their words turn out to be meaningless, if not outright false. We look to celebrities and athletes for help escaping from the slings and arrows of life, only to find that they are shallow, ill-informed, drug-addicted, banal, and care only about increasing their fortune and popularity. We read the most popular self-help books and follow the latest self-care fads, quickly setting them aside when something new comes along. Some look to organized religion for help, but increasingly find that the only return

---

2. https://www.brainyquote.com/quotes/tom_bodett_393824.

for an investment in time and money are pious platitudes and frequent invitations to contribute to the latest social justice cause.

Humanity needs hope. The institutional church has little or none to offer because it treats religion as a product to sell, not a means of support in the effort to respond to the challenge to grow in the expression of one's faith. I was a guilty as anyone of finding ways to excuse immoral behavior in myself and others. I would jokingly quote part of a verse from Paul's letter to the Romans where he asks, "Are we to continue in sin that grace may abound?" His answer in the next verse is an emphatic: "By no means!" But it was fun (or good for a laugh) to leave that part out for a second.[3] In my experience, many pastors are adept at turning a blind eye to sin when to do otherwise might cause conflict in the church. We ignore premarital sex, adultery, spousal and child abuse, cheating, deceptive business practices, and casual attitudes towards pornography to keep the peace or to keep the money flowing. We spend resources pontificating about social justice issues that impact a disproportionately small portion of the population while ignoring the poverty, crime, and moral degradation that impacts vast multitudes in our own backyards. Apparently, holding the right position is more important than holding the hand of one who is truly in need and helping lift them up out of the pit of despair. The institutional church, liberal, conservative, or middle-of-the-road, is far more concerned with right belief than right action. Every church is part of the problem insofar as it insists that salvation depends on adherence to the correct doctrinal assertion or social agenda over and above faith and trust in Jesus.

The words of Jesus and his earliest followers provide us with the way to attain the goal of "someone to love, something to do, and something to hope for." Translating this into Jesus' context yields the following: someone to love—God; something to do—follow Jesus; something to hope for—eternal life. Add to this the assertion that God will never abandon his children and you have the perfect recipe for joy and fulfillment. Best of all, what you need to learn about following this plan is found in the words of Jesus. The real challenge is not in reading and understanding what institutional Christianity promotes as the truth, but in setting aside the doctrinal propositions and assertions that have accrued over the last 1,600 years, propositions and assertions in which Jesus and his earliest followers would struggle to recognize themselves. True hope is found in a person, not a doctrinal pronouncement. I am not saying that every doctrinal assertion made by anyone other than Jesus is wrong. What I am and have been saying is that

3. "What shall we say, then? Shall we go on sinning so that grace may increase? By no means! We are those who have died to sin; how can we live in it any longer?" (Rom 6:1–2, NIV).

the doctrines the institutional Christianities of the West embrace were the result of fierce debates and the unnecessary shedding of Christian blood. Despite the claims of church councils, popes, and other leaders, salvation does not depend upon adherence to a set of propositions and neither does spiritual transformation. This was never Jesus' intent. True transformation takes place in the context of a relationship with Jesus, one that can only be realized in the context of community.

> At the time of the banquet he sent his servant to tell those who had been invited, 'Come, for everything is now ready.' "But they all alike began to make excuses. The first said, 'I have just bought a field, and I must go and see it. Please excuse me.' "Another said, 'I have just bought five yoke of oxen, and I'm on my way to try them out. Please excuse me.' "Still another said, 'I just got married, so I can't come.'"
>
> —JESUS[4]

The institutional mindset is not new in the religious realm. Judaism had its share of institutional religionists living in Jerusalem. Some believed that Jesus' teaching threatened their deeply held beliefs about ritual and doctrine. They feared he would delude people into believing that religious institutions were unnecessary. It is clear from the Gospels that Jesus did not advocate the destruction of the institution, several times encouraging people to participate in the rituals of the temple and the Jewish faith. Rather, Jesus objected to the assertion that rituals and doctrine were the only way to have a relationship with God. The dominant religious factions of the day focused on excluding from religious hope and practice anyone they deemed unworthy, not on helping them be worthy. Jesus made it clear that God extends the invitation of fellowship with him to everyone. This infuriated the religious authorities then for the same reason it does now: it denied their claim to absolute control over who was in and who was out. Jesus did his best to warn them, but instead of seizing the chance to transform a dead religion into a living faith, they chose to limp toward oblivion. The religion of Jesus, Second Temple Judaism—what we could call institutional Judaism—died when Roman-lit flames destroyed Jerusalem and the temple a generation after Jesus walked the earth. The institution died, but the Jewish faith remained and was a factor in the growth and development of early Christianities.

Jesus' compatriots failed to heed the warning he issued. They were too busy tending to their businesses to share in the joy of the master. Let

---

4. Luke 14:17–20, NIV.

me be clear: some faithful followers of Jesus, and even entire churches, responded to the invitation and walked in the way of Jesus, but some ignored it, distracted by the pageantry and pomposity of institutional Christianities both large and small, as is true today. We have a pope who is unwilling to dismantle the hierarchy in the search for justice for abuses visited by priests upon children and others over a span of many decades. He seems more agitated about capitalism and global warming than cronyism. Non-Catholic preachers all over the world draw large crowds of followers by proclaiming that praying yourself out of poverty is more important than helping the poor because, after all, poverty is a sign of sinfulness and divine displeasure. Where are the institutional Christianities that care about injustice? Where is the courage to call out other Christians and hold them accountable? There is none; there is only silence and the desire to remain unnoticed through the duration of the scandals. It is politically incorrect to claim the authority to correct others in matters of belief and religious practice if those beliefs and practices run counter to the notion that everyone is entitled to his or her version of the truth. As violent and nasty as the debates were, at least Christians in the fourth, fifth, and six centuries cared enough about the truth to be willing to fight and die for it. The losers may have gone out in a blaze of glory, but at least they did not quietly limp into oblivion. The same cannot be said for the institutional Christianity in the West today.

> "The servant came back and reported this to his master. Then the owner of the house became angry and ordered his servant, 'Go out quickly into the streets and alleys of the town and bring in the poor, the crippled, the blind and the lame.'"
>
> —Jesus[5]

The polemic of the previous paragraphs may lead some to conclude that I am eagerly awaiting the death of institutional Christianity. This is not the case. My hope is that it will discern what is necessary to get back on track and flourish. My fear is that it will do nothing, and its end will be the result. Institutional Christianity will not entirely disappear, but the expressions that are not persecuted out of existence will fade into the fabric of the culture and become irrelevant. The tragedy is that so many believe they can stay relevant by following the culture first and Jesus second. They sift his words to find what suits them and their agenda, ignoring whatever they deem inconvenient or outdated. Institutional Christianity claims to want to help the poor, the needy, and the hurting, but wants to do it on its terms, not those Jesus established. Institutional Christianity will help you so long as

5. Luke 14:21.

you are not so poor, crippled, blind, and lame that it becomes inconvenient, messy, and uncomfortable. It is easier to carry a sign in protest on behalf of the latest social justice cause or be welcoming and affirming to a tiny percentage of the population that rarely suffers from physical wants than to deal with the hundreds and thousands of children next door who starve to death every day for want of a little food.

The phrase "What would Jesus do" was wildly popular not many years ago, but it is largely absent from public view now. It was apparently just another religious fad, one that has joined the ranks of so many others. Books that Christians once bought by the millions to avidly read and discuss less than two decades ago can now be found in the deep discount bins at bookstores, on the shelves of thrift stores, and on the book table at rummage sales. Movies that once captured the hearts and imaginations of Christians and non-Christians alike suffer the same fate. Programs that sold for hundreds of dollars can now be had for pennies. Books and programs come and go, sometimes giving the people who read and use them a false sense of accomplishment. None last long because no matter how closely they follow the Bible, they are still developed by human beings. They can be good and much good can be done in and through them, but they are neither the source of eternal life nor the means to attain it. Worse yet, institutions and individuals rake in huge sums of money promoting their programs and selling support, which is then invested back into the institution. Nowhere in the words of Jesus do I find anything about living out the gospel and sharing the faith by developing programs. Regardless of how good the program may seem, think of how much good could be done with the money spent on these efforts. I am not suggesting that books, programs, and other resources be banned. I am suggesting that everything we do be measured against what it can do to carry on the mission of Jesus. Does it help the blind to see, the lame to walk, the sick to receive healing, the dead to be raised, and the good news to be proclaimed to the poor?[6] If not, then it is better off left undone.

I cannot escape the nagging feeling that what I wrote above is hypocritical. Perhaps it is, since the person who can escape any hint of hypocrisy is rare. Nonetheless, I am driven to write what I have written partly because I have kept silent for so long and partly because no one seems to be willing to point out the problem in its entirety. Institutional Christianity is dying in the West and being persecuted to death in the East. The end is coming. What will follow it? Is there anything we can do to stop it? I think I know.

---

6. Jesus replied, "Go back and report to John what you hear and see: The blind receive sight, the lame walk, those who have leprosy are cleansed, the deaf hear, the dead are raised, and the good news is proclaimed to the poor" (Matt 11:4–5, NIV).

Chapter 14

To Institutional Christianity:
A Modest Proposal

We have just enough religion to make us hate, but not enough to make us love one another.

—Jonathan Swift[1]

Jonathan Swift (1667–1745) is famous for satirically proposing that the people of Ireland sell their children to wealthy Britons for food as a way of recovering from the famine that was inflicting them. Swift (who was Irish) was attacking the heartless attitudes toward the poor that resulted when modern rationalism was used to solve the problem of poverty. His problem with this approach was that it treated people like objects rather than human beings with thoughts and feelings. Christians were taken in by the rationalistic notion that poor people were a problem to be solved, not a reason to reach out with compassion and love. Rationalistic religion, an essential element of institutional Christianity, is sporadically effective in changing beliefs and attitudes, but has little impact on the concrete expression of faith. Christians who are heavily invested in institutional Christianities seem to believe that their primary focus is to enforce doctrine. In some cases, this means enforcing the absolute doctrine that there is no absolute doctrine. Petty dictators abound amongst clergy and laity alike, but until recently few have had the courage to come out of hiding and openly declare their desire to rule. Instead, they twist Jesus' words about love into an excuse to hate and repudiate anyone who refuses to toe the party line. Some of the angriest church members I have met are people who claim they live their lives according the Jesus' command to love others, excepting of course those

1. https://www.brainyquote.com/quotes/jonathan_swift_385383.

who do not hold the same view. They use their view of Christian love as an excuse to hate, apparently without any sense of irony.

I am not in the same league with Jonathan Swift nor do I have his flair for satire. I am not in the same league with secular and religious scholars and intellectuals of the past and present. It is not my intent to present a detailed plan for church reform. I have no official claim to academic expertise, although I have read hundreds of books dealing with church history, theology, doctrine, worship, and evangelism. I do not have an advanced degree from a prestigious institution. I earned a bachelor of arts in Classical Latin and Greek from a small Catholic College. I earned a master of divinity degree from a Presbyterian seminary not highly regarded by graduates of elite institutions. I do not have a doctorate. I have spent nearly three decades among average Christians in average communities trying to serve Jesus to the best of their abilities. Through it all, I have kept my eyes open, watching what was going on around me as I both helped and hindered the cause of Christ. This leads me to what I am proposing should happen in view of the impending demise of institutional Christianities.

Swift's satirical proposal that the Irish solve their financial woes by selling their children for food is as shocking today as it was when it was written, but it makes a point the author may not have intended: new life requires sacrifice. This concept is deeply embedded in Jesus' message and call to action, but far too often ignored by his followers. Institutional Christianity is dying, but all it seems to want to sacrifice to survive are programs and employees. This tragically includes support for missionaries but does not include funding for efforts aimed at influencing the political positions of the United States of America. Mission and ministry are being callously sacrificed in the name of maintaining a voice in the political process. This is wrong on so many levels. What is more important: issuing a press release supporting a piece of legislation of dubious practical value to a tiny minority or using those resources to feed hungry children? Pontificate all you want about passing social justice legislation that will restore dignity to the oppressed, but the truth is that Christians fail Jesus when they cede personal responsibility for taking care of people to secular governments no matter how noble the legislation or sweeping the cause. Welfare in its current form would be called slavery in another age. Worse, it gives followers of Jesus an excuse to ignore our mandate to feed the hungry and clothe the naked. Political posturing requires little in the way of personal or meaningful sacrifice. Sharing what I have with someone in need is meaningful, and sacrificial, and it requires me to personally engage with that person. How sad it is that so many followers of Jesus believe that the taxes they reluctantly pay to the government and the rarely sacrificial monies they put in the offering plate are enough to fully satisfy Christ's call to action.

Institutional Christianity has been too accommodating to secular influences far too long, abdicating its divinely ordained responsibility to show compassion to those in need. This was not always the norm. Three hundred years ago the mainline churches on the frontiers of what was becoming the United States of America were still focused on preaching the gospel. This included inculcating in their adherents an expectation of benevolent action toward those in need. Two hundred years ago mainline churches were struggling to find their place in a religious landscape that increasingly featured intense personal conversion experiences and calls for social action as expressions of gospel faithfulness. One hundred years ago mainstream churches faced growing opposition from the scientific community as Darwinian theories gained traction in academia and the larger culture. Apologetics replaced action in the social realm, making doctrinal conformity more important than compassion for the poor and needy. Mainline churches occupy a pivotal moment in the history of religion, one filled with tension, ambiguity, and the struggle to remain relevant, but one ripe with possibilities for transformation and renewal of purpose. Institutional Christianity continues to be its own worst enemy, stumbling over self-created obstacles instead of moving them out of the way.

I am reminded of the (probably fictional) picture of the Emperor Nero calmly playing his fiddle while Rome burned down around him. Scandals plague institutional Christianity, but many of its leaders seem to want to act as if nothing is wrong. Roman Catholicism is bleeding to death from the countless atrocities inflicted against innocent children by pedophiles posing as men and women of God. Protestantism suffers from scandals both financial and sexual, accused of abusing the people it claims to help and protect. Silver-tongued charlatans spiritually and financially rape their followers in the name of God. Denominations and churches prostitute themselves to the latest social fad in the name of staying relevant but fail to attract new converts to the faith. Untold millions of dollars are spent building state-of-the-art campuses or renovating existing buildings to appeal to people of the right social standing and ethnicities. Congregations are deserting declining neighborhoods in droves in the name of looking for ways to increase numerical growth. Their fine new facilities lure people in with the promise of something wonderful to add to their already full lives while the poor in the places they deserted go away empty. They are building massive mausoleums for their members, not hospitals for the hurting. Is this what Jesus wants his followers to do? It is certainly not what he did.

Here is my modest proposal: Christian denominations and churches of every stripe must liquidate their assets—all of them—including buildings and furnishings—and sink every cent into helping the hurting. The church is a people, not a place. There are plenty of places available to gather on any given Sunday and if churches are doing what they are supposed to do there will be no shortage of offers. Dump the glitz, glamor, and technology and refuse to believe the lie that people will only respond to a message presented in media that appeals to them. Jesus reached people by the simple expedient of telling them that God cared about them and then showing them what that meant. There is no substitute for looking someone in the eye and telling him that God loves him and wants to help him of out of the mess he has created of his life. The fanciest media presentation will never replace the simple act of taking hold of the hand of someone whose life is spiraling out of control and telling her that God has a better plan for her life than she could ever imagine on her own. Technology has changed over the years, but human beings have not. The most basic human wants, desires, and needs have not changed. How dare we arrogantly assume that Jesus' method of reaching people is no longer relevant. People need people, not better technology, flashier media, or snappier presentations. The average church campus, as trendy as it may be, sits empty most of the week. We spend millions of dollars to cater to a crowd that shows up two or three times a week to be entertained and to take advantage of free childcare. What a waste! Get rid of the buildings, or better yet them to more useful purposes. Give the homeless a place to stay, feed the hungry, clothe the naked, care for the sick, help those released from prison to get back on their feet. Above all, do not insist that people assent to a set of doctrinal statements before receiving help. If that statement makes your head explode, then consider that nowhere in the Bible do I find any description of the last judgment that includes questions about doctrinal integrity, technological savvy, or the size of your church campus. Size does not matter; faithfulness is what is of the highest importance.

> As Jesus was leaving the temple, one of his disciples said to him, "Look, Teacher! What massive stones! What magnificent build-ings!" "Do you see all these great buildings?" replied Jesus. "Not one stone here will be left on another; every one will be thrown down."[2]

Speaking of exploding heads, when Jesus declared that the Jerusalem temple would be torn down, the resulting cacophony of bursting craniums un-doubtedly shattered eardrums for miles around. The denizens of Jerusalem

2. Mark 13:1–2, NIV.

were proud of their temple, believing that it represented God's choice to live among them in splendor. Even the rubes from Galilee who made up Jesus' inner circle were impressed by the magnificence of the temple complex. Yet, it was all for naught. The temple was destroyed, as Jesus knew it would be. The handwriting was on the wall in the form of factionalism, political unrest, and superficial faith. Rebellion was in the air, and the Romans were well-known for their scorched-earth policy in dealing with it. If the temple was the focus of rebellion, then the temple would be destroyed, never to be fully rebuilt again. Visitors to Jerusalem today can still see piles of massive stones at the base of the foundation wall. Jesus knew something his followers refused to acknowledge: Faith does not need a building, no matter how magnificent, to flourish and grow. Consider also that the Jerusalem temple represented an institution, one that sought to control not only the actions of individuals, but also to control access to God and therefore access to salvation. The destruction of the temple in AD 70 forced Judaism to redefine itself as a non-institutional religion. Christianity, although not yet differentiated to a high degree from Judaism at that time, also lived organically as scattered communities in all parts of the Roman Empire. I submit that this was its healthiest moment.

Unfortunately, it was not long before Christianities began succumbing to the temptation to build institutions designed to enforce conformity to one interpretation of Jesus' message against all others. The Jesus movement in its infancy was organic, fluid, diverse, and messy, but still of one mind as to the basics: "For God so loved the world that he gave his one and only Son, that whoever believes in him shall not perish but have eternal life. For God did not send his Son into the world to condemn the world, but to save the world through him."[3] How tragic it is that institutional Christianities are unwilling to proclaim this basic, essential truth. The reasons vary but come down to fear of giving offense. This is nonsense given that Jesus, Peter, and Paul, to name just three, made it clear that people would be offended by the proclamation of the gospel. It is part and parcel of the impulse to promote institutional survival above the truth. Some institutional Christianities have convinced themselves that the key to survival is inoffensiveness in the interest of filling seats and collecting enough money to meet budget priorities. Unfortunately for them, buildings, budgets, and agendas have nothing to do with the mission of Jesus and will not survive into the future, nor will they matter in eternity. The message of Jesus is clear: deeds mean more than decorative buildings or deftly crafted doctrines. Mainline Protestants go to great lengths to declare that deeds have no role to play in the attainment

3. John 3:16–17, NIV.

of salvation, but to write deeds totally out of the equation is a mistake. I believe the Reformers who formulated these ideas went too far in the name of wresting control of salvation from Roman Catholicism. Deeds do matter, as the words of Jesus make clear. They may not be the means of salvation, but they are a clear indication of where our priorities are located. I believe that Salvation is firmly rooted in the struggle between self-preservation and self-sacrifice. The former leads inexorably to death while the latter leads unerringly to eternal life.

> Jesus looked at him and loved him. "One thing you lack," he said. "Go, sell everything you have and give to the poor, and you will have treasure in heaven. Then come, follow me." At this the man's face fell. He went away sad, because he had great wealth.[4]

Some scholars believe that the man of great wealth in this story was Saul, who went on to become the apostle Paul. Whether or not this is true, the message for followers of Jesus is the same: faith in Jesus is more important than anything else. Faith is rooted in active action, not in passive assent to doctrines. Institutional Christianities in the Western world are dying because they refuse to put *true* compassionate action ahead of doctrinal assent. They refuse to take Jesus at his word. The resources tied up in church campuses, seminaries, denominational headquarters, and regional offices are better spent feeding the hungry than feeding institutions. Institutional Christianities pay lip service to the words of Jesus while doing everything possible to promote an agenda that assures their survival. Consider how the average church board would respond if Jesus showed up at the next stated meeting and declared that they needed to liquate their assets and use the proceeds to help the poor. I suspect he would face the modern equivalent of crucifixion. Wealth rules the Western world, not religion. Institutional Christianities no longer possess either the money or the cultural influence to make any sort of significant political impact on the world today. If nothing else, the scandals that beset institutional Christianities today make it clear that the ability to "speak truth to power" is severely diminished. It is no longer enough to reform the church, whatever that means. Instead, a complete rewrite of the operating system is in order. Start with the words of Jesus and move forward from there. Success as Jesus defined it is characterized by sacrifice, not institutional survival.

Jonathan Swift adeptly used satire to make his point, but there is nothing satirical in what I am proposing as the solution to the problems institutional Christianity faces. Some will opine that such a solution is

---

4. Mark 10:21–22, NIV.

impossible, to which I am compelled to respond with Jesus' words: "With man this is impossible, but not with God; all things are possible with God."[5] It is impossible for those so invested in the institution and its survival that they cannot see any other possibilities. I find it both tragic and ironic that churches with multimillion-dollar budgets dedicated to staff salaries, building maintenance, and technology bemoan the lack of funds to "do mission" in the world. Many of them have a "benevolence fund" dedicated to helping the needy, but my experience is that these funds often help people who have learned to work the system far more than they help people who are really in need. Helping pay someone's overdue rent or utility bill may be a good thing, but it rarely makes any lasting impact. There is so much more that the church could do to bring about positive change in the world. The truth that few are willing to acknowledge is that the resources needed to make a real impact on societal problems are there, but they are devoted to the wrong purposes. The American solution to many of these problems is to throw money at them, not to do what is needed to help lift people out of their circumstances. When will the church finally decide to care *for* people instead of just caring *at* them? It will only happen when Christians make the brave, dangerous decision to liquidate the vast assets of institutional Christianity and devote them to caring for people in ways that transform their lives and compel them to help transform the lives of others. This requires us to adopt a different attitude toward wealth and possessions.

The rich man in the parable quoted above went away sad because his possessions were apparently far more important to him than assuring himself of a place in eternity. Churches that place a higher premium on maintaining their buildings than on helping the hurting have their priorities in the wrong order. I served a church that adopted a policy of devoting 10 percent[6] of its operating budget to mission. This was done as a way of promoting the notion that the members should donate 10 percent of their income to the church. It was a nice idea but did not result in the intended outcome. Few people tithed to the church. The church budget was never fully funded by pledges even though, based on the incomes of the members, it would have been easy to reach that goal. Nevertheless, church members protested when this policy changed. The change was based on the idea that while giving money to mission organizations was a good thing, it was not as impactful as having people donate time and effort to supporting mission efforts in the local community and the world at large. What would happen if Christians banded together in communities and devoted 10 percent of

5. Mark 10:27, NIV.
6. This is known as a tithe, based on Gen 14:20.

their resources to meeting their own basic needs while devoting 90 percent to caring for the poor? Radical notion? Not really. Jesus suggested the same thing, but institutional Christianity dismisses it as impractical, unrealistic, or both. It goes away sad, because it has great wealth, and apparently that is more important than doing what Jesus wants his followers to do.

> It is rare to find an established community of Christians that encourages radical expressions of following Jesus. The natural conservatism of institutions is deeply rooted in the desire to survive, and that desire colors and limits the way they read the Bible and how they see God functioning in the world.
>
> —MICHAEL SPENCER[7]

The fundamental lie of institutional Christianity is that being a faithful follower of Jesus is nothing more than belonging to a group of like-minded people of similar social class and ethnic origin. In the not-too-distant past this also included a vague understanding of a common set of doctrinal assertions. While living in Christian community is an essential element of the faith, it is based on devotion to a person, not assent to a set of defined beliefs or identification with a specific ethnic or social group. It is true that there are basic assertions about Jesus that are essential to the Christian identity, but much of what is put forth as essential elements of faith are far from it. Institutional Christianities identify community as a value, but do not seem to understand what that really means. Community built on unity of purpose does not require unity of doctrine. The community of Jesus followers is built around faith in Jesus and his assertions, not assent to doctrines decreed after his death. If we truly want Christianity to survive into an increasingly dystopian future, then we need to accept that no one has the right to decide who is and is not a follower of Jesus. Radical? Perhaps, but I submit that a Christianity built on authentic community and compassionate action has nothing to worry about in the face of the demise of institutional religion in the Western world.

As difficult as it may be to contemplate, every institution is conservative, regardless of its political leaning, because institutions are focused on survival. They face the temptation to compromise their values in response to apparent threats to their ongoing existence. Institutional Christianity has given up on the idea of being radical, choosing instead to focus on being relevant in hope of conserving the institutions. What it fails to understand is that being relevant does not pay the bills. Established institutions, secular and religious, constantly put profit ahead of integrity. It is a slippery slope, one that leads

7. https://www.azquotes.com/quote/834557.

inexorably to perdition for all institutional Christianities. Someone will undoubtedly protest that the institution has a duty to take care of its employees.
This is nonsense given that institutions jettison employees at will in the effort
to keep the institution afloat. The truth is that the people at the bottom of the
institutional ladder lose their jobs first, which is one more indication that the
powers-that-be do not really care about those who need their jobs the most. It
should be noted that Jesus did not fire anyone—not even Judas—and that his
focus was on meeting basic needs, not on building an institution.

I am convinced that the values espoused by institutional Christianities have far more to do with corporate survival than transforming lives.
Progressives preach a message of tolerance and acceptance that offers little
hope or reason for authentic repentance and lasting spiritual growth. Conservatives preach a message of judgment and condemnation that offers little
hope of grace. Evangelicals try to steer a course somewhere in the middle,
but ultimately fail because their focus, despite all protests to the contrary, is
more doctrinal than relational and is aimed at maintaining and building institutions. The American definition of success means that even Pentecostals,
who may be closer to the spirit of the first generation of Jesus followers than
anyone else, focus more on building institutional empires than on creating
communities of believers devoted to caring for one another in authentic,
transformative ways. This is my point, one that I pray does not get lost in
the argument: Jesus wanted his followers to build organic communities, not
static institutions. Some will argue that this is an artificial distinction or a
distinction that does not need to be made, but I disagree. The church can
be *the* church without being *a* church, by which I mean a community of
Jesus followers that can carry out its mission without recourse to a resource-
consuming institution. Buildings do not build faith; people build faith by
sharing faith in the context of life. This does not mean sharing comforting
Bible verses and doctrinal assertions. Instead, it means personally coming
alongside the sick, suffering, oppressed, imprisoned, and poor to lift them
up out of their circumstances in the name of Jesus.

Other books have been written advocating a return to radical faith in
Jesus but as far as I know none of them suggest that such a return requires
the liquidation of the resource-hoarding bureaucracy that is Institutional
Christianity. Jesus followers will survive the demise of the institution, but
imagine how much good could be accomplished if the church made a conscious decision to die so that the Jesus movement could live. This is what
Jesus told his followers to do.[8] A supposedly Christian institution focused

---

8. "For whoever wants to save their life will lose it, but whoever loses their life for
me will find it. What good will it be for someone to gain the whole world, yet forfeit
their soul? Or what can anyone give in exchange for their soul?" (Matt 16:25–26, NIV).

on its own survival at the expense of its mission (as evidenced by budget-ary priorities) is not obeying Jesus' commands. Institutional Christianity will continue hemorrhaging members, here and there rallying a little, but its future demise is inevitable, accelerating with its shameless acquiescence to beliefs and values that run counter to the message with which Jesus en-trusted it. I do not claim to be a prophet, but it does not take a prophet to see the handwriting on the wall. The only question that remains is whether institutional Christianity will sink into its grave with a whimper or explode from the tomb with renewed energy and purpose, having shed its old bro-ken body and taken on a new, lighter form.

What is next? I am not a detail person, so I do not know what must happen beyond the broad strokes I have painted in this book. But I am sure that there are plenty of people who can figure it out given some time and a good dose of courage. Change is often perceived as death, and in a very real sense it is, but death makes room for new life. Such a change will be greeted with intense resistance by those who have invested more of themselves in the institution than they have in the mission of Jesus, which is a judgment statement, of course. But I stand by it because I am willing to be judged by the same standard. Protestant Christians recently celebrated the 500th an-niversary of the Protestant Reformation. There are interesting movements nibbling around the edges of Christianity, but none of them are doing much more than changing the paint and updating the curtains. Radical change is needed if Christianity is to be radically transformed. It is past time to make the main thing the main thing: feeding the hungry, clothing the naked, car-ing for the sick, visiting those in prison, and giving people real hope of an eternity where there will be, according to the promise of God, "no more death or mourning or crying or pain."[9] May that day come soon!

---

9. "'He will wipe every tear from their eyes. There will be no more death' or mourn-ing or crying or pain, for the old order of things has passed away" (Rev 21:4, NIV).

Scripture References

Cited and Referenced

Genesis 3:4
Genesis 14:20
1 Samuel 8:11–18
Psalm 23
Psalm 53:1
Proverbs 8:22
Isaiah 56:6–7
Matthew 6:19–20
Matthew 7:15
Matthew 7:23
Matthew 11:4–5
Matthew 16:16
Matthew 16:18–19
Matthew 16:25–26
Matthew 20:28
Matthew 23:24
Matthew 25:31–46
Matthew 26:11
Matthew 26:60–61
Mark 1:15
Mark 10:21–22
Mark 10:27
Mark 13:1–2
Luke 9:23
Luke 10:8–11
Luke 14:17–20
Luke 14:21
John 1:14
John 3:16–17
John 7:5

John 13:14–16
John 14:1–6
John 15:13
John 17:14–16
John 18:38
Acts 6:2–4
Acts 8:9–24
Acts 9:1–16
Acts 16:7
Acts 16:30–31
Acts 18:1–3
Acts 20:7–10
Acts 22:25–27
Romans 1:24–25
Romans 6:1–2
Romans 11:13–14
Romans 12:2
1 Corinthians 2:2
1 Corinthians 9:9
1 Corinthians 9:15
1 Corinthians 15:3–8
1 Corinthians 15:7–8
1 Corinthians 15:20
Galatians 1:11–16
Galatians 1:13
Galatians 3:28
1 Timothy 6:10
1 Peter 2:1
2 Peter 2:22
Revelation 21:4

Bibliography

Armstrong, Karen. *Muhammad: A Prophet for our Time*. New York: HarperOne, 2007

Chamberlin, E. R. *The Bad Popes*. New York: Barnes & Noble, 1993

Champlin, Edward. *Nero*. Cambridge: Harvard University Press, 2003

Estep, William R. *The Anabaptist Story: An Introduction to Sixteenth Century Anabaptism*. Grand Rapids: Eerdmans, 1996

Jenkins, Philip. *Jesus Wars: How Four Patriarchs, Three Queens, and Two Emperors Decided What Christians Would Believe for the Next 1,500 Years*. New York: HarperOne, 2010.

McGrath, Alister. *Christianity's Dangerous Idea: The Protestant Revolution—A History from the Sixteenth Century to the Twenty-First*. New York: HarperCollins, 2007.

Nietzsche, Friedrich. *The Gay Science*. New York: Random House, 1974.

Norris, Richard A. *The Christological Controversy*. Philadelphia: Fortress, 1980.

Orwell, George. *1984*. New York: Signet Classics, 1996.

Pavao, Paul F. *Decoding Nicea*. Selmer, TN: The Greatest Stories Ever Told, 2014.

Reese, Willy Peter. *A Stranger to Myself: The Inhumanity of War: Russia, 1941–1944*. Translated by Michael Hoffmann. New York: Farrar, Straus and Giroux, 2003

Rose, Michael S. *Goodbye, Good Men: How Liberals Brought Corruption into the Catholic Church*. Washington, DC: Regnery, 2002.

Rubenstein, Richard E. *When Jesus Became God: The Struggle to Define Christianity During the Last Days of Rome*. San Diego: Harcourt, 1999

Shelley, Mary. *Frankenstein*. London: Penguin Classics, 2018.

Walton, John H. *The Lost World of Genesis One: Ancient Cosmology and the Origins Debate*. Madison: IVP Academic, 2009.

Subject Index

Note: n indicates footnotes.

Scripture Index

CPSIA information can be obtained
at www.ICGtesting.com
Printed in the USA
BVHW041204181019
561475BV00016B/2091/P